SO-AFS-083

2014

The Idealware

FIELD GUIDE

to Software

for: Nonprofits

....

A Quick Guide to Essential Software for your Organization

Welcome

The *Field Guide to Software for Nonprofits* is very much a labor of love for Idealware. For more than eight years, we've researched the software that can help nonprofits more easily pursue their missions. We've interviewed countless nonprofit staff members on hundreds of different topics to gather the impartial information that organizations need to make better decisions, and spent thousands of hours analyzing it to create easy-to-understand overviews.

The Field Guide is the culmination of our work, summarizing all that information into a handy, easy-to-use publication. Through straightforward overviews, it helps nonprofits pinpoint the types of software that might be useful for their needs and provides user-friendly summaries to de-mystify the possible options.

Idealware has grown, and so has the Field Guide. In this annual update, our fifth edition, we've carefully updated all the information included in the previous versions and added a number of new emerging tools, technologies, and practices and specific aspects of nonprofit software—we've also added an entirely new section that guides you through the sometimes daunting process of *Choosing and Implementing Software* (beginning on page 187).

We know you have your hands full creating incredible outcomes for your clients and communities, and don't always have time to keep up with the latest information about the software that can help your organization. That's where Idealware can help. Thank you for all you do to make the world a better place. We hope this Field Guide will help you do it all just a little more easily.

Laura S. Quinn
Founder and Executive Director, Idealware

TABLE OF CONTENTS

MORE RESOURCES

What types of software would be helpful for your nonprofit in the areas of back office productivity, collaboration, fundraising, and outreach and communications? The *Field Guide* is designed to answer exactly that question.

This Introduction helps you understand how to use this guide, walks you through the software we believe every nonprofit organization should have, and provides an overview of a few key terms.

Ready to think through the types of software your nonprofit is likely to find helpful? Dive right in...

This Introduction walks you through the software we believe every nonprofit organization should have, regardless of size or mission, and provides an overview of a few key terms that apply to nonprofit software.

The Case Study section provides an overview of the different types of software used by a set of fictional—but plausibly realistic—nonprofits. If you're unsure what you might need, this is a good place to start. These examples can help you pinpoint the specific types of software to investigate further in the next section.

The remainder of the guide is organized to help you find the types of software that might be useful based on the goals you're trying to achieve. We'll walk through the software designed for seven different areas: Back Office and Productivity, Listening and Measuring, Collaboration, Constituent Management, Fundraising and Events, One-Way Communications, and Two-Way Communications. In each section, we'll first take an overall look at the types of software that might be useful based on your own situation and your organization's level of technical sophistication. Each section then contains an introduction to the software types that might be useful in that area—nearly 100 different types of software in all.

Note that some systems overlap different areas. For example, *Page Layout* software can be considered part of both the Back Office and Productivity area and the One-Way Communications area because of the different ways in which an organization might use it. In those cases, we included the full description of the system in the area in which we think they fit best for their primary use, but also refer to them in other sections.

The final section, Choosing and Implementing Software, walks you through the process of selecting the best tool for your budget and needs and putting it to use at your organization.

We recommend that you begin with the case studies or the walk-throughs for each category to identify the types of software you're likely to find useful. *Every time you see a software type high-lighted like this,* it means we covered it elsewhere in this guide, so you can refer to the appropriate section for more information. Having trouble finding something? Consult the Index at the back of the book for a handy reference to all the types of software covered.

Where did all this information come from? At Idealware, our mission is to provide information to help nonprofits make smart software decisions. Over the years we've done impartial research and reviews of many different types of software. This Field Guide is the synthesis of all that research—it boils thousands of pages of reports and articles down to a handy, concise guide. But of course we couldn't do it alone. Dozens of nonprofit technology staff and consultants reviewed this Field Guide content to make sure it was accurate and useful. At the end of the book, you can learn more about the Idealware staff and generous reviewers who made the Field Guide possible. ●

Systems that help with such common tasks as managing constituents and maintaining websites can benefit nearly every organization, regardless of mission or budget.

Back Office and Productivity

Whatever your mission, there are certain tools you'll need to manage your organization and staff day in and day out. If you have more than one staff member, an Excel spreadsheet is not going to suffice for accounting purposes—you'll need a dedicated *Accounting* system to track finances, expenditures and payroll.

Office Software is important to help you create and edit documents, spreadsheets, presentations and all the other materials on which organizations run. *Email and Calendar* software lets you and your staff send and receive critical emails and share your schedules. You'll need an internet connection to support email, obviously. And if you have an internet connection you need *Virus Protection* software to keep malicious computer viruses and spyware from compromising your data or your productivity, and increasingly, a *Firewall* to prevent hackers or others from gaining unauthorized access to your data and computers.

Finally, you'll need a *Data Backup* solution to protect your organization's data and save you the time, cost and effort of recovering from a data loss.

Listening and Measuring

Whether it is widespread or confined to a single social network, if your organization has an online presence you should be monitoring the impact you're having and seeking opportunities to join conversations about your mission or cause. You should also be listening to and adapting to feedback from constituents or other people with whom your organization interacts.

Collaboration

Whether you have two staff members or two thousand, you need some way to share and manage files with each other and with the other people your organization interacts with. A good *File Sharing* system won't break the bank, but will make your life noticeably easier.

Constituent Management

Most fundamentally, you'll need some kind of software to track donors, event attendees, volunteers and other constituents. Excel spreadsheets are great for maintaining a family task list, but quickly show their weakness when you begin tracking even just a few complex interactions, such as donations. A good database should let you store all the information you'll need about all your supporters.

What type of system will best help you will depend on your specific needs and budget. There are a number of basic types, each ranging widely in cost depending on the features you want. Every organization needs some type of system—a *Donor Management, Constituent Relationship Management, Association Management, Case Management or Volunteer Management, or Integrated Online System,* or even a *Specialized Constituent Management System*—but which one makes the most sense for you depends on your specific needs. (See the Constituent Management section for more information.)

Systems that help with such common tasks as managing constituents and maintaining websites can benefit nearly every organization, regardless of mission or budget.

Fundraising and Events

Of course, it's important for every organization to raise funds—and to do that well, you'll need some kind of system to track constituents, and effective ways to reach out and engage people, as covered in the next section.

One-Way Communications

In addition to tracking constituents, it's important to have a website that clearly communicates who you are and what you do. In order to easily update your website yourself with new information or events as they happen, regardless of how technical you are, you'll need a *Web Content Management System* (CMS). Unfortunately, it's not easy to add a CMS into an existing site, but almost every organization should consider using one when building a new site.

You should also have a *Broadcast Email* package designed to send out emails to hundreds (or millions) of people. Email is a quick and cost-effective supplement to direct mail or face-to-face communication, and a great way to reach out to or engage constituents or to fundraise, but it's important to have a different tool for your *Broadcast Email* than you use for your individual emails.

Two-Way Communications

Building and maintaining a base means going beyond reaching out to new constituents but engaging them in long-term, ongoing relationships and conversations. There have never been so many options, but which ones you choose will depend on your specific audience and needs. ●

How can different types of nonprofits most effectively use software? This section provides examples of how fictional-but-realistic organizations use software to meet their needs. It starts with smaller organizations that aren't yet ready to make a big investment in software, and then moves to larger organizations with more complex needs.

All of the software names highlighted within the text are covered in more detail in this guide—look them up to learn more.

Shoostern Music History Society
Just Getting Under Way

One Staff Member/$100,000 budget

Less than a year ago, the Shoostern Music History Society received a seed grant to create a nonprofit organization around a single gift. The gift—hundreds of music instruments—came from a benefactor with a deep interest in the history of music. The nascent Society provides historians and scholars with access to the collection, and supports research on the history of music.

The seed grant will support the Society's single employee, Julie, for a few years—enough for her to get everything up and running. It won't last beyond that, however, meaning that fundraising is a top priority. The Society also needs to reach out to its local community, and nationwide, to let scholars interested in antique instruments know the collection is available for study.

Julie started with the basics. She knew that she'd need *Office Software* and tools to support *Email and Calendaring,* as well as a way to track their finances in a straightforward *Accounting* system. She uses a free *Virus Protection* and *Firewall* software and inexpensive online *Data Backup* to ensure the safety of the organization's contacts and other materials—though the Society is small, their information is priceless.

With her software infrastructure in place, she began her fundraising process by creating lists of possible individual donors, foundations and scholars in Excel spreadsheets. Before long, she realized the spreadsheets would make it difficult to track multiple donations and the small, but important, number of scholars who were also donors.

She spent about $400 for *Donor Management* software that can track all the people with whom she interacts. It's made a huge difference—she imported all the Excel spreadsheets she'd created with no trouble, and can easily find people, enter gifts, and create lists of people she needs to call or mail. She considered a *Constituent Relationship Management* system, but decided she didn't actually need much additional functionality beyond what a donor management system could do—why deal with the extra complexity and setup of a more complex system?

Now she's looking at ways to keep constituents engaged. Many of them are academics, and an *Email Discussion List* would let them keep in touch with each other—and with the Society—about issues of mutual importance. She also knows the value a good website can bring to an organization, so she hired Matt, a consultant, to build the site. She chose Matt primarily for his experience with free *Web Content Management Systems*—he showed her how to use the software to update the site's text and images so that once the site is built she can keep it fresh.

Julie is working toward adding an online "virtual tour" of some of the instruments in the Society's collection that highlights the heart of the organization. *Photo Editing or Multimedia Editing* software would make it easier and more affordable for her to do things that she would have needed professional-caliber tools for just a few years ago. Given that many of the Society's constituents and community members are academics, she's thinking of asking them to help find the content for the tour using *Crowdsourcing* techniques, and *Collaborative Documents* to collect and manage their input. She's also exploring a free *Wiki* site to help her community edit information about the collection. In addition to using their expertise and knowledge to make creating that content easier, Julie thinks this strategy will help keep her constituents engaged and excited about the organization.

She also created a *Facebook* page for the organization, and tries to spend at least two hours a week posting updates, but since her constituent-base is not likely to seek out a more steady social media presence from the organization, she's relegated such actions to a lesser role. Because so many of the researchers who avail themselves of the organization's resources maintained *LinkedIn* profiles, she created a discussion group through the site that links them into an informal community where they can share conversations about the collection. She also uses *Online Conferencing* to "meet" with experts from around the world in informal video conferences to seek their advice and input on the Society's collection.

What's next on the software front? Julie's considering the best way to create a newsletter—initially she wanted a printed news-letter, and looked into *Page Layout* software to help create it, but now she's leaning toward an email newsletter. If she had a solid *Broadcast Email* package she could use it to send not only eNewsletters, but email appeals, as well, killing two birds with one stone. *Online Donation* tools would help her handle the resulting gifts and pledges. She's also prioritizing online *Foundation Grant Research* to find other grant opportunities to help keep her organization in existence once the seed grant runs out.

She's confident that with the right software she'll be able to successfully run the entire organization and serve her audience well, despite being the only staff member. That's music to her ears. ●

Kids' Collective
Building Up Fundraising and Communications Infrastructure

Eight Staff Members/$800,000 budget

This is an exciting time for the Kids' Collective—the organization just received a $100,000 grant to increase the number of children it serves with afterschool service-learning programs. Eager to use this momentum to grow fundraising and outreach work, the eight staff members rely on an army of volunteers to deliver many of the organization's programs, which means a lot of feet-on-the-ground work and scheduling to coordinate, and a lot of people to organize.

A few years ago, Joanna, the executive director, made the decision to invest in a *Constituent Relationship Management* system (or CRM) to manage all their key constituents—the kids in the programs, their parents, donors, volunteers and more. Since there's a lot of overlap between these groups—for instance, parents often volunteer or donate, and some of the kids have even grown up to put their kids into the program, creating a second generation—Joanna wanted to be able to get a full view of specifically how each person is involved. This made a CRM system a better fit than either a *Donor Management* system, which couldn't easily track their program participants, or a *Volunteer Management* system, which was too narrowly focused. She also considered a *Specialized Constituent Management System* like a *Student Information System,* but didn't find the systems she demoed flexible enough for her needs. The system also provides basic *Broadcast Email* and *Event Registration* functionality, integrating these online components while eliminating the need for additional software packages.

Kids' Collective does have a separate *Online Donation* tool, though. Their development director exports data from that system, and then imports it into the CRM system to sync the two.

The *CRM* Joanna chose provides great functionality for communications and fundraising—it's easy to email an eNewsletter to subscribers each month, create labels to mail paper newsletters, and support quarterly appeals. And she worked with Eric, the organization's communications director and "accidental techie," to set up an *Email Discussion List* that lets board members, major donors and core supporters discuss ideas for the organization. The list has turned out to be a bigger-than-expected success in understanding what's important to those groups, and engaging them with ways they can help.

As it's important to the organization to proactively understand what its community wants, Eric installed a *Web Analytics* package to get a sense of what Kids' Collective events and resources people found most interesting on the website. Since people also talk about such things online, he's using *Online Listening* to monitor those discussions as well as circulating an *Online Survey* to more proactively check in with staff and kids via a quarterly survey. They've discussed using a *Dashboard* to make it easy to see all of these different metrics into one view, but they're not sure if it would be worth the time to set it up.

A lot of the Collective's programs are based around specific events—for instance, a big volunteer-kickoff day to encourage high school kids to join a longer-term service program. The organization does a lot of promotion to cast a wide net for these events, both on- and offline. A *Web Content Management System* makes it easy to post events and information about them on the organization's web page, but Joanna and other staff post on social networking sites too—particularly *Facebook,* which is pretty widely used by the kids they work with. They use it to promote specific events, but it works to publicize the organization, as well. Using *Event Registration* software, kids can RSVP to events. This streamlines the process somewhat, but it's always a little hit-and-miss to try to figure out who's coming.

The events involve a lot of coordination as well, and staff relies on a number of different back office and collaboration tools to help keep everyone in synch. They couldn't function without

Email and Calendaring software, and an online tool provides *File Sharing* functionality to allow both staff and volunteers to access documents from wherever they are. They also use a simple *Intranet or Portal* to post information, dates, and contact information for all the team members.

Joanna invested in professional-caliber *Page Layout* software, and her team creates posters for schools and community centers. Not coincidentally, the software's also great for laying out newsletters. Photos are a critical tool for the Kids' Collective to help show kids in action in the organization's newsletters, on the website and in promotional materials. Eric convinced Joanna that they didn't need anything fancy in this area—in fact, free *Photo Editing* software meets all their needs in editing photos for print or the web, and they can share whole libraries of them online using *Photo Sharing Websites*. The kids love seeing pictures of themselves and often post their own on Instagram, a *Niche Social Networking Site* beloved by young people. Based on some of the emails Joanna receives, it turns out adults love seeing their own pictures taken at events, as well.

When Joanna noticed how many of the kids had their own cell phones—and how many of their parents used them to keep in touch—she worked with Eric to help her optimize their website for visitors browsing on smartphones, which was much easier than creating a separate *Mobile Website* while meeting many of the same goals. They've also begun to use *Mobile Text Messaging*, taking advantage of a communication method almost ubiquitous with teens to remind their kids about volunteer events.

In the short term, Joanna wants the kids in the program to participate in more events, but she's also hopeful that as they grow older they will become volunteers and donors themselves, passing on all that they have learned. ●

Seeds of Hope
Telling Their Story Online

Six Staff Members/$1.5 Million budget

U.S.-based Seeds of Hope uses seed grants and training to help former child soldiers in Africa earn a sustainable living, often through farming. The nonprofit relies on technology more than many, existing as a sort of "virtual organization." Not only are most of its constituents on another continent entirely, but the handful of staff members are spread out across the United States. Lawyer David Landis started the organization after spending time volunteering in Africa. He recruited other staff members based on their skills rather than their location, and invested a portion of the seed grants in technology to facilitate a remote workforce, knowing it would also enable the organization to eventually serve constituents around the world.

Ensuring all the staff members can share information from wherever they are is a challenge. They decided that a straightforward *File Sharing* solution wouldn't let team members search and find information like they needed to, so they decided to invest in an online *Document Management* system that lets anyone easily archive and retrieve files from anywhere. They also use more straightforward *Collaborative Documents,* especially to work on documents together in real-time. *Screencasts and Screenshots* and *Online Conferencing* tools also let them share information visually across the world. David is researching a *Learning Management System* to help train his far-flung staff, but isn't sure the organization needs quite one yet.

The organization relies on individuals in the States for a portion of its funding, and for their help advocating for effective U.S. aid policies. This means the organization must reach out to and connect with potential donors and supporters all over the world in a variety of ways.

David leveraged the organization's early results by posting individual success stories of former child soldiers on Seeds of Hope's website each month and fleshing them out with compelling photos and videos. He invested in a strong *Web Content Management System* that lets him and his team upload and format these posts in intuitive ways. David's coworker, Heidi, took a few classes to learn the basics of a professional level *Photo Editing* package. Now she can edit photos sent from the field and format them for the web or print publications. In addition, by posting photos to *Photo Sharing Websites,* she helps a wider audience find their stories. David tracks *Web Analytics* to see which stories are of most interest to site visitors, so he can tailor future updates accordingly.

Some of the most popular posts are videos recorded in the field. They found that the videos don't need to be incredibly sophisticated or expensive to work—Heidi learned to use free *Multimedia Editing* tools to cut and join video clips, and to add titles, credits and voiceovers. She posts them on a *Video Sharing Website,* which provides free video hosting, and then embeds the videos on Seeds of Hope's own site—these combined methods distribute videos to a wider audience than either method alone. Staff has also been experimenting with adding their stories onto *Social Content Websites* to try to draw in a different audience.

These success stories have worked so well that the organization's recently begun to build around them for education, outreach and fundraising. Three staff members in the field have started *Blogs* that follow a few of the people introduced in these stories and videos. In addition to reaching new audiences, the blogs keep those interested updated on the former child soldiers' progress over time. It's a great way to keep people engaged with the organization's issues and work, and with the organization itself.

They find *Maps and GIS Systems* as well as *Charts and Diagrams* to be invaluable in showing the need for, and impact of, their work. On their website, they show frequently updated maps of the regions with the most former child soldiers, overlaid with information about the people and communities that they've helped through their programs and services. And they've recently hired a graphic designer to put together an infographic that highlights this information in an easier-to-read format that can be easily shared through social media, like *Facebook, Twitter,* and *Social Content Websites.*

David and other staff are also trying different online outreach methods to help put these stories in front of new people who might care about them. They use *Search Engine Optimization* to boost traffic to the website, invest in targeted *Online Advertising,* and experiment with social networking sites—primarily *Facebook,* which reaches a broad swath of interested people, and *Twitter,* where David posts a number of times a week or whenever he finds links to disseminate. *Online Listening* and *RSS* help them understand what people are saying about Seeds of Hope.

Of course, the core goal of the success stories is to move people to action. With each story, web visitors find a call-to-action prompting them to join an email list, and the organization holds a number of fundraising and advocacy campaigns every year to encourage list subscribers to take action. Information about donors and activists is stored in an *Integrated Online System,* which replaces the need for separate *Broadcast Email* and *Online Donation* software. Each year, David also encourages supporters—especially younger ones—to help raise money through *Peer-to-Peer Fundraising,* and to give via *Mobile Text Messaging.* They've even recently developed a *Mobile App* that provides timely news to their followers and lets them know how they can help. Seeds of Hope is also exploring putting up a project on a *Crowdfunding* platform to let supporters help it reach a tangible goal.

As important as money is, the organization's supporters play another role as critical advocates for effective U.S. aid that can support Seeds of Hope's mission. David assigned a staff member to manage *Petitions and Pledges* and tools for *eAdvocacy* to encourage supporters to act in favor of critical aid reform.

Thanks to technology, location no longer makes a difference—but Seeds of Hope and the people behind it do. ●

Springfield United
A Fundraising and Outreach Powerhouse

35 Staff Members/$3.5 Million Budget

For half a century Springfield United has supported and helped grow the city of Springfield. A six-person fundraising team works to raise money through a wide assortment of campaigns, special events and grant support, and distributes it where it will do the most good.

The headline event is Springfield Days, a two-week fundraising push held each May that includes a publicity campaign and walk-a-thon, culminating in a gala dinner and auction. The logistics are daunting, but sophisticated software makes managing them possible. The Springfield United team uses *Event and Auction Management* software to manage the complicated gala arrangements, including the seating plan and the on-site live auction. *Credit Card Processing* systems let them accept credit cards for auction purchases, saving staff the hassle and extra paperwork of the carbon copy imprinter they used to use. Using *QR Codes* posted with each auction item, attendees can use their smart phones to quickly and easily learn more about the local businesses and sponsors who have donated. The team also uses an *Event Registration* tool to help sell tickets online. There's an online component, as well, which the team runs using *Online Auction* software.

Every year Springfield United screens a new "Faces of Springfield" video at the gala to showcase the organization's work and the strength of the town. Team members used to outsource the video production to professionals. The past few years, however, they've begun producing the video in-house using *Multimedia Editing* tools.

A major focus of Springfield Days is the Saturday walk-a-thon. Many supporters have participated for years, raising money from their friends and family with their walk. For the first time last year, the organization also tried using an online *Peer-to-Peer*

Fundraising component for the walk-a-thon, which worked well. Some supporters were more comfortable creating their own online fundraising pages to reach out to people they know, rather than asking them in person. Others enjoy throwing their own events for the cause—the organization's *Custom Online Community* lets supporters talk with each other and share tools that work.

Despite the success and popularity of Springfield Days, fundraising and outreach isn't just a two-week affair. Recognizing this, the team mounts various campaigns and appeals throughout the year. A robust *Donor Management* system lets them manage a series of direct mail appeals and a substantial foundation-grant outreach effort. They've integrated their database with an *Integrated Online System* to handle the online side of things, including email appeals and online donations and additional functions like managing website content. The fundraising team is also considering adding a *Mobile Text Messaging* component to the mix, to send text messages to subscribers—providing yet another way to reach out to potential donors.

Major donors are a big part of the organization's fundraising. To reach them the organization first created a core "major donor" team made up of development staff, board members and a few committed volunteers. Since team members work in disparate locations, the organization facilitates their work with collaboration tools. First, *Email and Calendaring* software set up in conjunction with a server lets them trade email and share their schedules with one another. An *Email Discussion List* and regularly scheduled *Online Conferences* allow them to trade strategies and keep in touch. Collaborative Document tools let them work together on shared materials, and an Intranet gives them access to shared organizational resources.

Project Management Software lets each team track its progress and manage each member's responsibilities and deadlines, which makes working from different locations nearly seamless.

The organization has recently identified a need to better manage staff members, payroll, and hiring, so they're considering a *Human Resources Management System* to streamline that process and free up the time spent on human resources. Up until now, the Executive Director has been managing employee data using Excel spreadsheets, which worked sufficiently when the organization was much smaller, but as the number of employees has grown, so have its needs.

Like the staff, the board of directors—key to the organization's continued success—is made up of busy people who are rarely in the same location. *Board Collaboration* software lets members communicate with each other and with the executive director, and makes sure they have the right materials to review and comment on as well as a regularly updated calendar of board- and organization events.

Springfield United is also using *Social Media* to reach out to its audience. Staff members are experimenting with *Online Listening* to help understand what people are saying about the organization and its issues, and have started a *Facebook* and *Twitter* presence to engage new supporters and inspire them to donate or volunteer. They're trying *Online Advertising* on websites and blogs that cover topics related to their mission. In addition, the organization tried an online *Pledge,* encouraging people to "Buy Springfield" to support local stores and producers. The experiment went well—thousands of people signed the *Pledge.*

At a young staff member's suggestion, the organization is considering adding a *Geo-Location* component to some of its bigger events to let attendees "check in" at the gala or post their progress at the walk-a-thon.

Overall, staff has found that the best software approaches help them to harness the passion and energy of the people of Springfield—something the city has in abundance. ●

Wooster Hall

Engaging the Community in the Performing Arts

42 Staff Members/$2.8 Million budget

Wooster Hall's mission is simple—bring high quality performing arts, including music, dance, opera and theater, to the community. Over time, the small organization has built up a committed base of subscribers and donors. Now it's targeting new audiences, hoping to build the next generation of subscribers.

The performances are at the core of Wooster Hall's activities, and the majority of marketing and outreach is focused around them. The staff—led by Rachel, a former dancer with a lot of connections in the arts—carefully plans, lays out and mails a quarterly pamphlet of upcoming events, and keeps the website up-to-date with detailed information about each show. *Page Layout* software and a sophisticated *Web Content Management System* make these tasks easy and efficient. It's a challenge to manage all the images from so many events, along with the rights information, so the organization recently invested in *Digital Asset Management* tools to help.

Rachel also works with staff on *Search Engine Optimization* and *Online Ads,* putting careful thought into keywords to ensure that people searching for arts events in the community find Wooster Hall's performances. She posts to *Facebook* and *Twitter,* using the social media channels to share photos from performances and to post information about upcoming events. Friends and followers repost these announcements, which helps reach new audiences who may not otherwise be familiar with the performance series. To cover all her bases, she's also posting to *Niche Social Networking Sites* dedicated to the arts, and even created a place page for the theater using *Geo-Location Tools* to let attendees "check in" at arts events as a means of building interest. Simple *Social Media Measuring* tools let her track the traffic and response her posts get, showing that collectively, her social media efforts provide a good return on investment in terms of advertising.

Informing new audiences isn't enough, though. The Wooster Hall team works hard to engage people who have attended past events to maintain and grow their interest. Those who've attended an event are more likely to come to others, and much more likely to volunteer or donate—they're an important segment of the organization's audience. In the past couple of years, Rachel and the staff focused more and more of their efforts online. They posted clips of performances to *Video Sharing* and *Streaming* sites to let fans relive moments and forward them to friends, and they package the best speakers and music into a monthly *Podcast* series—10-minute shows subscribers can listen to in their cars or on their iPods. Jerry, the outreach coordinator, is a good writer, so he keeps a *Blog* featuring his "backstage" take on events. The blog has proven very popular—in fact, that the organization is planning a series of live "Online Salons" where Jerry will interview arts personalities while participants listen over their computers and post questions they'd like him to ask using *Online Chat*.

Rachel is also working with some of the artists to create *eLearning* modules that teach a little bit about their particular media. The more people learn about the arts, the more interested she hopes they'll be in attending performances, and today's new students are tomorrow's performing artists.

Ticketing software integrated with the organization's website lets staff sell tickets to events; box office staff can access the software as well to coordinate seating. Development staff then pull data for fundraising appeals. Most fundraising is done in two yearly appeals, conducted by both direct mail and email. A robust *Donor Management* system helps staff manage the details, including basic *Broadcast Email and Online Donation* functionality. And with a *Point of Sales* (POS) System, they can manage transactions, track inventory, and process credit card payments from the concession stand and gift shop.

To keep constituents happy, Rachel carefully monitors feedback about performances and what people would like to see in the future. In addition to keeping an eye on the local media for reviews, she uses *Online Listening* to keep abreast of what people are saying online. This has become such a useful feedback loop that she created a *Dashboard* using RSS to make it easy to see a summary page of who's saying what. She also periodically surveys subscribers using *Online Surveys* to better understand what shows they'd like to see.

Wooster Hall recently received a grant from a local foundation to increase its presence with underprivileged members of the community, who haven't historically been part of the organization's core audience. As that grant winds down, Rachel's overseeing a major *Program Evaluation* effort to gauge its impact. Her staff is using software to *Analyze Paper Data* to make sense of notes from focus groups and interviews with audience members, and *Statistical Analysis* and *Custom Reporting Tools* to make sense of the quantitative data they have collected.

Of course, all the technology hasn't made Rachel forget the best way of getting feedback from constituents—Rachel never misses a performance, and before and after each event, she's in the lobby shaking hands, mingling, and talking with the people who make her job possible. ●

Every nonprofit, regardless of its mission, needs a set of software tools to help with day-to-day work. From Office Software to Photo Editing to Document Management systems, these tools can help you be more efficient and effective.

All of the software names highlighted within the text are covered in more detail in this guide. Most of them are included in this section and follow immediately after the descriptions.

If you're interested in a software type and can't find it in this section, you can look it up in the Index.

In addition to the *Accounting, Office Software, Email and Calendar, Virus Protection, Firewall*, and *Data Backup* systems covered in the Every Organization Needs section, software designed to help with the day-to-day activities of any organization can make your work more efficient and hassle-free.

....

Strongly Consider...

You probably use photographs for your website, richly formatted emails or any other newsletter or communication—people love them. If you use photos taken in the field or at events by staff, volunteers, or constituents, chances are you've wanted to edit them from time to time—say, to remove red-eye, improve the lighting, or crop out unwanted features. *Photo Editing* software, once the domain of the professionals, is now a standard tool for even the most amateur of photographers.

Page Layout software can help you design and lay out those same materials, including newsletters, emails, pamphlets, brochures, flyers, posters, or any other number of printed and online materials.

If you want to take users' credit card information for member-ships, donations, purchases, or other transactions, you'll find a number of affordable *Credit Card Processing Systems* and *Point of Sale Systems* that can make such tasks painless and secure.

Keeping Ahead of the Curve...

Once you realize how easy editing photos can be, you might want to try editing video or audio—both excellent ways to engage constituents. *Multimedia Editing* software makes these kinds of challenges easy and affordable.

Larger organizations can create a considerable volume of docu-mentation. It's a lot easier to create than to store and manage this output, especially when you go back to find something later. *Document Management* can help you keep the mountains of materials under control and within reach.

Larger organizations may want to explore dedicated *Human Resources Management* software to keep track of hiring, benefits, and lots of other tasks related to your most important resource—your own staff.

On the Cutting Edge...

Documents are not the only things that can grow unmanageable—images, presentations, audio clips, and other files pile up quickly. *Digital Asset Management* offers a way to archive, search, and retrieve such files. ●

Accounting Systems

If you're managing more than a few thousand dollars at a time, you almost certainly need an accounting system. Even if you have help with accounting—maybe bookkeeping, payroll, or someone to help out at tax time—you still need a solid system to track and manage revenues, expenses, payments, and other finances.

Conversely, even if you have a good accounting system, you still need some knowledge of accounting. If you lack that knowledge, consider hiring a bookkeeper to set up the software so that it does what your organization needs it to.

Lower-end systems starting at a few hundred dollars will work fine for most organizations with one or two accounting users and budgets of up to $2 million. QuickBooks is popular and relatively easy to get up and running, and there's a cloud-based option too—Sage 50 (formerly Peachtree) can offer more flexibility, but assumes some accounting experience. Others, like FUND E-Z by FUND E-Z Development Corporation, are designed specifically for nonprofits and provide functionality of interest to nonprofits who need to track money in and out of complex funds.

Organizations with more than four or five users or budgets over $2 million might consider more complex systems. At this level, the cost of implementation can sometimes exceed that of the software. Nonprofit-specific systems in this realm include Sage 100 Fund Accounting and The Financial Edge by Blackbaud.

Not all organizations need systems created specifically for nonprofits. General business accounting packages, like Microsoft Dynamics and Sage 100 ERP, tend to be more widely used, which makes it easier to find help with setup, support, and bookkeeping. They can also track inventory, billable hours or other relevant data, and offer support not provided by most nonprofit-specific packages.

Accounting is a complex area, and there are a lot of high-end systems available. If you manage hundreds of millions of dollars, more than a hundred staff, or a complex, multi-unit national or international structure, seek expert advice on enterprise systems. ●

For more info, visit
www.idealware.org/accounting

Don't Forget Payroll...

Nonprofits with multiple full-time staff members (rather than volunteers) are going to need some way to manage payroll, time, and attendance. Small organizations might look to Intuit's Online Payroll (formerly PayCycle), while mid-sized organizations might look to ADP (Automatic Data Processing) and time-tracking tools like Kronos. The smallest nonprofits may be able to manage these processes through Excel or Google Spreadsheets.

Credit Card Processing

Want to take payments via credit cards? It's neither difficult nor expensive to do.

Many nonprofits are starting to process credit cards on smart-phones or tablets. This ultra-portable method uses a mobile device with a data plan or Wi-Fi to process transactions by letting you either manually enter card numbers or, with the addition of inexpensive hardware, swipe cards directly. Square, Intuit's Gopayment, and PayPal Here can support mobile payments. Third-party card readers are available, and range in price, but both Square and PayPal provide readers for free. Some fundraising software vendors, including Sage, also support mobile payments.

Online payment processors, including Click & Pledge, Greater Giving, and GiftTool, allow you to process credit card payments (such as online donations, event registration, or item purchases) over the internet, typically for a $20-$40 monthly fee and a small percent of the transaction. These vendors typically provide an interface optimized for your constituents to submit payments on their own, but most of these interfaces work perfectly well to allow your staff to process payments, as well.

Alternatively, many mid-tier and advanced *Donor Management* software packages, like DonorPerfect, eTapestry, and The Raiser's Edge, let you process donations and other payments directly from that software. This convenient option lets organizations process a high volume of a single type of payment, and saves time-consuming double-entries.

If you need to take credit cards on-site and a mobile payment processor isn't practical, you can use an imprinter—those small machines that swipe and carbon copy the credit card so you can charge it later—or you could invest in a credit card terminal, also called a "swipe terminal." These terminals let you swipe a credit card, enter the payment amount on a keypad, and then process the payment over a phone line. You can typically get either of these pieces of hardware from the bank that holds your merchant account or rent them for a particular event from such sites as Auctionpay.

If you want to take credit cards in a permanent physical location such as a gift shop, registration desk or cashier station, you'll need more hardware. *Point of Sales* software, like CAM Commerce Solutions or Keystroke POS, can integrate it all and help you manage actual inventory. ●

For more info, visit
www.idealware.org/creditcards

Data Backup

A backup strategy serves two purposes—to allow you to retrieve files that were inadvertently deleted or changed, and to let you recover from a disaster. Backup software helps implement this strategy by copying data from its original location on a computer's hard drive to some sort of storage media. Traditionally, backups are recorded onto a physical device, like a tape or separate hard drive, and then stored in an external location outside the office to keep your data safe in the event that a disaster—like a flood or fire—destroys your office.

Local backups are primarily physical solutions, like a USB data key or a tape drive, used to back up an entire server or drive. Software applications such as Symantec's Backup Exec, Apple's Time Capsule, or Windows' built-in backup utility allow administrators to schedule local data backups so they happen automatically.

Remote backups, which allow you to copy your files to an internet-based data storage location, are an increasingly popular option. The best backup strategy might be a combination of both on-site and online solutions. Since it can take significantly longer to restore data from a remote backup than a local one, having both options can give you the flexibility to recover quickly from minor mishaps while also protecting you from catastrophes.

Remote backup tools like Amazon Simple Storage Service (S3), MozyPro, Jungle Disk, IDrive, and Carbonite offer affordable, easy-to-use software interfaces designed to back up desktop and laptop computers to cloud-based storage. Though all backup solutions should be monitored, these packages don't require the level of care and feeding typical at the enterprise level. What you typically give up, however, is centralized management and monitoring. Other tools, like Egnyte.com and Box (formerly Box.net), go beyond the basics to provide online enterprise-class replacements for traditional hardware file servers by storing your files and backing them up at the same time.

Specialized devices, like those made by Datto and Barracuda Networks, or solutions like CA's ARCserve, provide both on- and off-site backups through networked storage drives programmed to also back up its contents on vendors' servers. Designed for IT professionals, these packages are powerful, but can be daunting for staff without a technical background.

Even with the best backup software, data backup is a notoriously temperamental procedure. It is important to perform data recovery tests regularly to ensure that your information can be restored when needed. ●

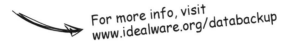

For more info, visit
www.idealware.org/databackup

What should you be backing up?

The simple answer? Everything. Or at least, everything that's critical, valuable, irreplaceable, or important to your organization. Consider each of your organization's processes separately and account for each by identifying and backing up its data. And remember—backing up file servers won't do any good if individual staff members are storing their valuable data on local hard drives. Make sure networked computers all have access to file storage, and that everyone on staff is using it.

Digital Asset Management

Many nonprofits manage a lot of digital assets, including photos, audio and video files, and PDFs. *Digital Asset Management* software helps organize, categorize, and track data about these files—for example, setting permissions for certain files, managing rights, and tracking usage—and allows a number of people to find and share files.

If you only have a couple hundred multimedia files and don't need to track complex information about them, free online tools like *Photo Sharing Websites* and *Video Sharing Websites* might suffice. Other sites, like Box (formerly Box.net) or Smartbins (formerly Wonderfile), store and share any kind of file. They'll let you upload, share, and tag files, but aren't likely to support complex organization schemes or track tons of data. Microsoft SharePoint is a more powerful, flexible option for internal file management, and is available at a discount through TechSoup. Many *Web Content Management Systems* also have useful functionality in this space.

There's a whole class of system dedicated to managing photo and video files, including Extensis Portfolio Server and NetXposure DAM. These tools help multiple people organize, share, and track photos. At the top-end of the market, sophisticated products like OpenText eDOCS OpenText, KIT digital, Virage MediaBin, and Canto's Cumulus can cost tens-to-hundreds-of-thousands of dollars.

More concerned about tracking documents or a whole range of file types? You'll find sophisticated options for those needs, as well, often called *Document Management Systems.* ●

For more info, visit
www.idealware.org/dam

Document Management Systems

Is your organization drowning in a sea of documents? *Document Management Systems* (DMS) can help you find and manage all the documents your organization uses, from staff memos and publications to invoices.

For small organizations with a reasonable level of document output, simply organizing the files and folders on your file server can provide a basic level of document management. Even adopting a naming system can make a difference—for example, naming a document "Jones Fax 05-13-08.doc" instead of "Jones. doc" is a rudimentary form of managing documents by making it easier to find them later. (Free search solutions like Google Desktop, Copernic, and Windows Desktop Search can help find documents, as well.)

Larger organizations of 50 or more employees, or those with a particularly heavy document output, can benefit from a *Document Management System* that provides searching, versioning, comparison and collaboration, workflow integration, and metrics that reveal how your organization uses your documents.

For simpler needs, affordable *Document Management Systems* are often resold with photocopiers and scanners. Primarily intended as image and PDF management systems, they can also manage files created on the network, and your organization may already have one. These bundled *Document Management Systems,* like Laserfiche, may not include the very high-end features offered by an enterprise-level system, but will offer the basics, and often come with very competitive, tiered pricing.

Microsoft SharePoint is another popular choice. SharePoint integrates with Microsoft Office documents, and offers sophisticated workflow and routing features and extensive document- and people-searching capabilities. This powerful tool is expensive, but available to qualifying nonprofits for a low administrative fee through TechSoup, which offers both SharePoint Standard Edition and Enterprise Edition. There's also an online version. Other affordable options include Alfresco and KnowledgeTree, both free, open source tools. A few cloud-based options include SkyDrive,

Apple's iWork for iCloud, and even Google Drive. All of these packages will likely require considerable setup time and some technical know-how.

For more money, but less work, a number of systems like Questys are geared specifically to support document management processes for mid-sized and larger organizations. At the high end of the market are a number of sophisticated systems designed for large organizations and corporations, including Open Text eDocs, Autonomy WorkSite, and EMC's Documentum. ●

 For more info, visit
www.idealware.org/dms

Email and Calendar Software

Microsoft Outlook and Google Apps are the most common email solutions in the nonprofit world, and both tie users' email and calendars together. While these tools may serve different purposes, the combination allows staff to easily share their schedules with each other.

Outlook is the client side of a client/server package from Microsoft. When paired with Microsoft Exchange, it becomes a feature rich application offering email, calendar and other functionality. This reliable choice is often familiar for users, and provides as much advanced functionality as you're likely to need. It's also inexpensive through TechSoup (just $5 per user for Outlook, and $45 for Exchange, though you'll need someone with technical know-how to set it up and maintain it).

A number of organizations, including Microsoft itself, can provide an online hosted version of Exchange for a monthly fee—a useful choice for organizations without IT staff. This option allows your staff members the convenience of either hosted or installed Outlook for email and calendaring, but replaces the need to buy and maintain a physical Exchange server. Google Apps offers an increasingly compelling alternative to the Exchange-Outlook combination. This suite of tools includes email, shared calendaring and documents, and more, and is free to 501(c)(3) nonprofits. Though Outlook's features are more robust, Google Apps focuses instead on providing solid functionality to meet most typical user needs. Administration is streamlined, easily supports information sharing, and has sophisticated built-in Spam filtering.

Other software packages like Mozilla Thunderbird and Zimbra offer free, open source solutions targeted at email management for individuals. Optional add-ons provide calendaring functionality. ●

The Name Game

You'll need to register a domain to use any organizational email tool. Using the same domain for your organizational email accounts (george@idealware.org) and website (www.idealware.org) is inexpensive, looks more professional, and is easier for people to remember than using free email domains like gmail.com, yahoo.com, or hotmail.com.

Use an online domain registrar to see if a particular domain is available—NetworkSolutions.com is the most widely known example, but sites like Register.com, NameCheap.com, easyDNS.com, and Gandi.net are cheaper—and lease the rights to the domain for $10 to $20 per year. Someone with a bit of technical savvy can use the tools provided by your registrar to point your new domain to your email software package. It's worth noting that some registrars are better than other at protecting clients from false takedown notices. If your work is controversial, read up on the registrar's policies regarding domain security. Do they shut down first and ask questions later when a business or government takedown request comes in?

You might also explore domain registrars with built-in, easy setup options with third party software, like iwantmyname.com—this particular tool allows for low-cost domain leasing and built-in setup options with Google Apps and ZoHo.

For more info, visit www.idealware.org/emailandcalendar

Firewalls

A *Firewall* is a virtual barrier between your machine or network and the outside world. It guards against intrusions from hackers and malware, which is a generic term for the many different forms of malicious software. *Firewalls* work by monitoring both incoming and outgoing traffic, and by letting you restrict what gets in and out.

A good *Firewall* includes predefined settings that let common traffic take place unimpeded—otherwise, users need to approve every transaction, which would be both overwhelming and annoying. They should also enable you to white- or black-list specific IP addresses or hosts, approving or denying access on a permanent basis. A *Firewall* that runs in stealth mode makes the computers it protects invisible to hackers and similar threats. More advanced *Firewalls* can inspect all information from the internet for evidence of intrusion into your systems, attempts to disrupt access to them and filter out files that are likely malicious.

Network based *Firewall* appliances protect your entire organizational network by inspecting traffic from the internet and screening out malicious activity or information before it reaches your computers. A firewall appliance may be as simple as a home/office router from D-Link, Linksys, or Netgear, or as sophisticated as the products from Cisco or SonicWALL. Prices vary widely depending on features and functionality. A low-end firewall appliance can be bought for under $200, while a high-performance device from Cisco or SonicWALL can run several thousand dollars.

Firewall software installed on individual computers can provide machine-level protection that a firewall appliance can't. For example, a laptop without its own *Firewall* might be safe while connected to your protected organizational network, but will be vulnerable when connected to an unknown wireless hotspot.

Many desktop *Firewalls* also let you block pop-ups or banner ads, encrypt credit-card information, or protect passwords—features which may be useful to your organization. Newer versions of Windows include a built-in *Firewall,* and Norton and Kaspersky both offer trusted third-party *Firewalls* that are included in their internet security suites. ●

For more info, visit
www.idealware.org/firewalls

HR and Office Management

Human Resources Management Systems and human resources information systems—commonly abbreviated as HRMS or HRIS—can reduce administrative time and improve efficiency by helping your organization track and organize its human resources data. How do you know that you need an HRMS? Conventional HR wisdom holds that you generally need one HR manager for every 100 staff members—that ratio holds true for your software, as well. Keep in mind, though, that even if you have only 30 or 40 staff members and no HR staff, an HRMS can save a lot of time that can be used for other projects.

If you don't have a dedicated HR department, or even a staffer whose sole duty is to manage human capital, you're not alone. Many nonprofits don't, and rely on employees who have responsibilities in such other areas as administration, finance, or operations to take on HR as well. If this is the case, you'll need a user-friendly system that doesn't require a lot of upkeep, so that the software really is a time saver for the employee who uses it.

At its most basic, HR management just requires a place to keep all your employee information. It's quite possible to roll-your-own solution, using Microsoft Access or FileMaker databases to manage employee demographic, contact, and compensation information, or even just keeping track in an Excel spreadsheet or a Google Doc.

You may also find it possible to adapt your existing payroll software, like Intuit's Payroll Services or PayChoice. These options both integrate with Intuit's QuickBooks accounting software, and can provide functionality to keep track of benefits, employee demographic information, and compensation history, and could serve as a useful repository for employee data in lieu of a more sophisticated system.

Once your organization grows past a few dozen employees, you might want to consider implementing a more-advanced solution, like ADP Workforce Now or Sage HRMS, which can handle more complex timekeeping issues. For the largest organizations, you may need an enterprise-level solution, like Kronos, Ceridian, or Oracle's PeopleSoft.

You may also consider a smaller, specialized solution targeted at managing only a specific subset of HR. These include Cyber Recruiter and iCIMS for hiring and recruitment, and Visual Staff Scheduler for scheduling. These tools can be used in conjunction with one of the smaller, less feature-rich solutions in order to meet a specific HR management need without resorting to one of the more expensive enterprise solutions. ●

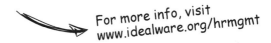

For more info, visit
www.idealware.org/hrmgmt

Multimedia Editing

Multimedia Editing software gives you the capability to create videos or Podcasts with a level of a polish that used to require a lot of expensive hardware. Good editing takes time and some skill, but a number of low-cost, straightforward packages put the tools within reach of any nonprofit. There are lots of free and low-cost mobile apps and web-based software that nonprofits can use, too.

With audio packages, you can edit interviews for length, cut "um"s and pauses, and add music or voiceover introductions. Both GarageBand (for the Mac) and Audacity are free, solid tools that provide all the functionality you're likely to need.

Video tools let you cut out footage you don't want, splice different sections together, and overlay graphics and text onto your piece. You might join an interview with a constituent together with scenes of your program participants, and put a title screen and music at the beginning—and with a single click, even upload the video to YouTube or Vimeo. It is possible to over-edit your video. All of the software options we discuss come with special effects that can enhance your video, but don't overuse them—a little goes a long way. Consider tools that help you make short videos like Vine, Viddy, and Instagram Video, too.

For Mac users, iMovie (free with the Mac operating system) is a great editing tool for simple movies. The free editing software available for PCs, on the other hand—like Windows Movie Maker and Pinnacle Systems' VideoSpin—can be difficult to work with, and often imposes insistent front-and-center ads or confusing limitations on supported formats. Alternatively, for friendly features very similar to iMovie, consider Premiere Elements ($22 for nonprofits on TechSoup, or about $49 retail).

If you've outgrown the low-cost options, or want to create more robust animations or special effects, Final Cut Express and Final Cut Pro provide logical stepping stones for Mac users, while Adobe Premiere is a popular option for both Macs and PCs. These products, all under $1,000, provide a lot of power. If you're skilled- or savvy-enough and have high-end video production needs—and a budget to support them—there are numerous video solutions available on the market. Avid Technology makes the most well-known, including the core of its product suite, Media Composer, which costs several thousand dollars and requires a powerful computer to run it properly. If your need for video editing is sufficient enough to need such tools, you're likely better off contracting a professional video editor.

Once you've edited your movies, it's easy to get them up onto the web—see *Video Sharing and Streaming* for more information. ●

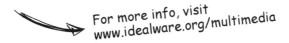

For more info, visit
www.idealware.org/multimedia

Want to Produce a Free, Easy Inspirational Video?

If you're looking for an easy way to turn your photos and video clips into inspirational videos, consider Animoto. It helps you to upload your images and clips, lets you select some music, and then automatically turns them all into a music video-style montage. If you don't like the first one it creates, you can just ask it to create another one—each one is different.

Office Software

Office Software helps with the day-to-day tasks that keep an organization running, including creating and editing documents, spreadsheets, and presentations. There are three primary options for nonprofits: Microsoft Office, open source suites like LibreOffice or Apache OpenOffice, or an online solution like Google Drive. Apple shops can use iWork, too.

Microsoft Office is the default choice for many nonprofits. With its sophisticated feature-set, familiarity for many users, low price for most nonprofits through TechSoup, and integrated online file sharing in more recent editions, it makes sense for the majority of organizations. With the newest version of its software, Office 2013, Microsoft has begun to more heavily promote use of Office 365—a distinct edition which moves the Office suite away from single-user software installed on desktops and into multi-user services accessible via the cloud.

The free and open source LibreOffice and Apache OpenOffice are no more complicated to install than Microsoft Office, with a feature-set and interface similar to Microsoft Office 2003—which is to say, not quite as snazzy as Microsoft's newer releases. They also lack some of Microsoft Office's very advanced features, but is a quite usable alternative, especially for a small, technically comfortable staff philosophically aligned with open source tools. (If you're still upgrading from Office 2003, LibreOffice and Apache OpenOffice might even be an easier transition than the redesigned ribbon interface Microsoft introduced in Office 2007.) LibreOffice and Apache OpenOffice are very similar to each other in features, and both trace their roots to the original OpenOffice project; the former generally has a more active developer community than the latter, and tends to release updates and patches more frequently.

The third option is not to use installed software at all, but an online suite like Google Drive, Zoho, or ThinkFree. Google's free tools provide a straightforward, friendly set of features to cover the core needs of business users, offering functional-if-limited, features to create, edit, and share documents. Zoho and ThinkFree (both of which have free versions, but for most functionality cost around $50 per user, per year) offer more advanced functionality, but neither provides the sophisticated functionality or features of Microsoft Office.

For most organizations, switching completely to online office software probably doesn't make sense, as the tools aren't likely to be sophisticated enough to make it worth the learning curve. But online tools can be tremendously helpful for documents that require a lot of input from a number of different people, and can be useful as supplemental tools for producing *Collaborative Documents.* ●

For more info, visit www.idealware.org/officesoftware

Page Layout

Page Layout software enables you to arrange design elements (like text, images, colors, and lines) to create newsletters, posters, reports, invitations, and other materials. Appealing layouts require graphic design skill as well as software, but good page layout software can make your job easier and put high-quality designs within reach of anyone willing to learn a few basics.

Straightforward projects such as reports or text-heavy posters can often be designed in word processing applications (Microsoft Word, Google Drive, or OpenOffice.org Writer, for example). These tools offer more control over fonts and images than you might think, but lack the flexibility to handle multiple design elements, complex text flow, and spacing, and don't offer complex professional printing options. Microsoft Publisher, part of the Office Professional package, offers more sophisticated control—it's also more straightforward than full-fledged layout software, but isn't nearly as feature rich.

Unlike word processing applications, professional layout software treats pages as a series of distinct elements, and lets you format, edit, or rearrange them independently of one another. Feature-rich tools like Adobe Creative Suite 6 ($20 through TechSoup), Adobe InDesign Scribus (free and open source), and QuarkXPress can be used to design anything from posters and newsletters to full magazines, books, or newspapers. Mac Pages is an option for Apple users.

If you struggle with multiple columns, images, and page numbers using a tool like Microsoft Word, professional page layout software can be a revelation. They'll also speed up the layout process tremendously. But the complex menus and tools make these packages difficult to learn. In many cases, you'll need a solid foundation in graphic design lingo to understand their terminology. Investing in a good book or taking a class will get you on the right track. ●

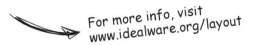

For more info, visit
www.idealware.org/layout

Photo Editing

Digital cameras have put professional-quality photos within everyone's reach, but once you've got a high-resolution image, how do you prepare it for print or the web?

Cropping—trimming an image to remove unwanted items or to isolate the subject—is often needed to make a photo look professional. Color correction—for example, boosting a washed-out photo's color, or removing red eye—can save a less-than-perfect image. And resizing can make an image the appropriate dimensions for the target media and shrink file sizes to make websites load more quickly.

The right *Photo Editing* software can do all these tasks and many more, but tools in this area are often a trade-off between power, usability, and price.

As the cameras in smartphones and other mobile devices improve, more people are using them to take pictures. As such, there's a wide variety of free and paid apps to help manipulate your photos. Instagram is a popular tool that lets users apply various filters to photos and upload them to an online profile, but other apps like Camera Plus and Adobe Photoshop Express offer more control. For Android users, PicSay, Vignette and Photoshop Express are strong options.

Free tools aimed at the home user or small business, like Google Picasa, iPhoto, Adobe Photoshop Express, and Pixlr, are simpler to use than professional applications. Most provide plenty of functionality for simple image-correcting and cropping, but don't support advanced features like multiple image layers, or the ability to cut a person out of a background and paste them into a new location.

Middle-of-the-road packages like Adobe Photoshop Elements or Paint.NET add additional power, but also additional complexity. Web-based tools like PicMonkey and Photo Collage are free and offer the ability to do some creative work with your photos.

Adobe Photoshop ($20 for nonprofits through TechSoup as part of Creative Suite 6) is the most widely used professional-caliber software in this field. GIMP, a free and open source program, offers many of the same features in a somewhat less-intuitive interface. Even tech-savvy users will benefit from some form of instruction on these packages, whether through a book, a class or one-on-one time with a graphic designer. ●

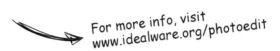

For more info, visit
www.idealware.org/photoedit

Point Of Sales Systems

If your organization has a public storefront—like a museum with a store or gift shop—you'll need a good point-of-sale system to help you manage purchases.

Point of Sales, or POS, systems help manage the transaction between buyer and seller, and typically support physical rather than online storefronts. Far more than just a cash register or credit card processing machine , POS systems consist of various combinations of software, hardware, and services to keep track of everything from items, prices, taxes, sale date and time, discounts, and payments. A POS system will also handle returns and exchanges on items as well as voided transactions—some can even provide inventory management and sales reporting. The mobile boom has transformed the *Point of Sale* landscape; for much more on processors that work with phones and tablets, see the *Credit Card Processing* section.

Some organizations will still need to use traditional POS software. Popular all-in-one solutions include Intuit's Quickbooks POS and Microsoft's Dynamics POS and Dynamics RMS. These systems will provide your core POS needs at their base prices, and more expensive versions will add more robust features, like employee management, support for multiple stores, or integration with e-commerce solutions. These systems will also integrate with widely used accounting systems, like Intuit's QuickBooks, Microsoft Office Small Business Accounting, or Sage 50 (formerly Peachtree).

In addition to these tried-and-true installed systems, there are also a number of newer, cloud-based solutions available, like Posterita, ZingCheckout, and Cashier Live. Because there's no software to install, these systems are easy to setup, more easily integrate multiple storefronts or social media channels, and provide more support for mobile devices.

While these systems already mentioned are intended for more general small business consumers, several products exist that are specifically designed with nonprofits in mind, like Blackbaud's Altru and Cougar Mountain Denali. These tools, while more expensive, provide robust all-in-one support, and may include a constituent database (to manage your customer, volunteer, or member records, for example), or are offered bundled with hardware like cash registers, price poles, or receipt printers to help nonprofits get their storefront set-up more easily.

A good POS system will make transaction-related tasks easy, allowing you to focus on the bigger picture of managing your organization's retail presence and interacting with customers. ●

For more info, visit www.idealware.org/pos

Virus Protection

Antivirus software seeks both to stop malicious software—known as viruses or "malware"—from reaching your computers, and to "disinfect" them of malware that might be installed. While antivirus software is typically installed on individual laptops and computers, there are also solutions designed to protect email servers and file servers.

Norton, Trend Micro, and McAfee are popular desktop antivirus solutions, but many nonprofits are turning to the free versions of such packages as Microsoft Security Essentials, Avira, AVG, and avast!, all of which also have paid versions. Mac users can use MacKeeper. Keep in mind that paid antivirus software often offers centralized management, which can be valuable for organizations with more than a few computers to protect.

Antivirus applications should offer real-time protection by monitoring machines around the clock, scanning incoming and outgoing emails and attachments for viruses, and quarantining any they find. Make sure the antivirus solution you choose will integrate with your email client, if it's not web-based.

You should also be able to schedule periodic updates to let the software download new virus definitions to protect against all current-known threats. Automatic updates are particularly helpful for organizations with multiple employees who might not all remember to run updates manually.

While antivirus solutions for regular file servers are typically the same as those for desktops and laptops, email server antivirus usually requires an additional cost module that scans and cleans messages before making them available to users. The goal is to keep danger as far away from your users and systems as possible.

To this end, many organizations now use cloud-based email antivirus solutions by vendors like Postini and MessageLabs to detect and clean any infected email messages before they reach the network. Some hosted email solutions, like Google Apps, will include this automatically. ●

Don't Forget the Human Element.

Virus Protection doesn't stop with software—your staff members have to use their common sense, like not opening suspicious emails. It's also important to change passwords regularly, and create more secure passwords (stay away from "password" and "1234"). Password management services, like LastPass or IronKey, can make it easier to manage and remember a large number of complex, unique passwords.

For more info, visit www.idealware.org/av

Do you know what people are saying about your nonprofit online? Are you tracking conversations you could be involved in, asking your constituents for feedback and opinions, and adapting your efforts to the response they generate? Listening and measuring are becoming increasingly critical practices for organizations.

All of the software names highlighted within the text are covered in more detail in this guide. Most of them are included in this section, and follow immediately after the descriptions. If you're interested in a software type and can't find it in this section, you can look it up in the Index.

Effective communication isn't just about talking—it's also about listening to what your constituents are saying, asking their opinions, and checking in regularly to see what's working and what's not. Using the right tools can help you manage your message.

∙∙

Strongly Consider...

If you track constituents in a *Donor Management* or *Constituent Relationship Management* system (described in our Constituent Management section), think through the information you'll need to collect in order to know which techniques are working. How did you initially connect with each constituent? What communications have they received? What actions have they taken with your organization? Have they donated—and if so, how much, and in response to what appeal?

This information can help you refine your methods over time. Straightforward metrics can also tell you a lot about how your communications are working. *Web Analytics* can provide very useful information about how many people visit your site and what they're doing there. Similarly, *Broadcast Email* software, profiled in our One-Way Communications section, can tell you how many are opening your email, and what they're clicking on.

Chances are people are talking about you whether you ask them to or not. Just as organizations can use a clipping service that collects their mentions in print media, *Online Listening* lets you search for online mentions and alert you to their presence. But it can be useful to proactively ask people what they think, as well. Such traditional research techniques as focus groups, interviews, and user-testing work well, but *Online Surveys* provide a particularly quick and often very effective way to gather data. *Email Discussion Lists* let you ask quick questions of a group of core supporters.

If you're using social media, you should be measuring your success and adapting your efforts to what you learn. *Social Media Measuring,* either through the channel itself or with third-party analytics software, can track and report on all kinds of useful information.

Keeping ahead of the curve...

When you're ready to go beyond what *Online Listening* can easily offer, *RSS* offers sophisticated ways to monitor the web, filter out what's most useful to you, and create a *Dashboard* to summarize it. It's also useful to participate in relevant *Social Content* and social networking sites where you can hear what people are saying and sometimes ask questions directly.

Program Evaluation can help you better track the information you need to improve the effectiveness and efficiency of your programs. Software can help you track and analyze the data you'll need, but in order to make any meaningful conclusions, you need to first carefully identify certain things. Many nonprofits track much of their data at a client level and then roll it up across multiple clients to help them better understand the broader impacts of their programs—but if you're tracking things that aren't specifically related to particular constituents, you may need a different database, or to start using your existing database differently.

Maps and GIS software is becoming an increasingly user-friendly and practical means of seeing where your supporters are concentrated, for example, or where your programs are having an effect.

On the cutting edge...

Organizations that want to stay proactively on top of what their constituencies want and think can create advisory boards to help provide input and feedback. While these advisory boards can often function very successfully through in-person meetings, conference calls, or via email, it's worth considering software that might help the group collaborate, like *Custom Online Communities* or *Wikis* (both covered in the Collaboration section of this guide.) If a major research or evaluation project has you drowning in physical files, you might consider tools to help with *Analyzing Paper Data* or *Statistical Analysis Tools* to identify quantitative trends.

If you are tracking and acting on a range of metrics, it can quickly become overwhelming. *Custom Reporting Tools* might make sense for complex analysis. A *Dashboard* also lets you collect metrics in a single, easy-to-view manner and make it more efficient and effective to monitor them. ●

Analyzing Paper Data

Nonprofits that are surveying constituents or gathering client-reported data might find it impractical or too expensive to use software to do so, especially when working with populations that are unfamiliar with or unwilling to use *Online Survey Tools*. Using paper forms to collect information is cheap and easy at the point of collection, but what can you do once you're faced with a mountain of paper surveys that all need to be analyzed?

One solution is *Optical Character Recognition Software,* or *OCR Software*. OCR is a process by which handwritten or printed text can be digitized into a computer using an external scanner. That image is then converted to machine-readable text that can be searched, analyzed, and/or imported into your database. OCR programs can be fallible, especially when dealing with messy handwriting or nonstandard fonts, but their accuracy has improved vastly in recent years. Still, staff members may need to take the time to check over the scans and correct them manually as needed.

New scanners often come with basic OCR Software. If you're looking to scan large numbers of documents at once, look into a dedicated document scanner with a feeder that can allow you to scan whole stacks of paper at rates of up to 150 pages per minute. The staff time this can save you might be worth the investment.

If you're on a tight budget and have a newer scanner, consider freeware OCR Software, like OCRFeeder, FreeOCR, Tesseract GUI, or TextRipper. Additionally, if you use Microsoft Office, you may already have Microsoft OneNote installed.

Once your paper data has been scanned and digitized, you'll need to analyze it—in the case of surveys, to identify trends. Sociologists, anthropologists, and other academics who use Qualitative Narrative Analysis to conduct their research often rely on tools called Computer Assisted Qualitative Data Analysis (CAQDAS) to discern patterns or trends from pages of text. Qualitative Narrative Analysis Software (or QNA Software) auto-mates the coding process through user-defined "story grammar" that assigns categories and values to narrative content.

Proprietary software can be very expensive, and could be of limited use to a nonprofit that only needs to analyze a few hundred interviews. Major players on the market include NVivo, ATLAS.ti, and QDA Miner from Provalis, which also offers a free and fairly robust version of the software in QDA Miner Lite.

Open source CAQDAS tools are often developed and supported by universities. Coding Analysis Toolkit, a web-based system from the University of Pittsburgh, is a free and fairly user-friendly option for users with basic needs. Qiqqa is described as a "reference management software" and helps manage and analyze information stored in PDF documents—and also includes a built-in OCR process. If you're conversant in the programming language R, and hope to use it to analyze your data, RQDA is an R package designed for Computer Assisted Qualitative Data Analysis. Like R itself, it's free and powerful, but you'll need to understand the coding language to use it. ●

What about Analyzing Audio or Video?

If the information you're trying to analyze is primarily in the format of digital audio or video that hasn't yet been transcribed—from in-person interviews, for example—your options are slightly different. Transana doesn't transcribe your multimedia files automatically, but relies on user assistance to generate transcripts from which qualitative data can be coded and analyzed. It is an open source tool, but does carry a relatively small fee—about $65 per user, or $500 per multi-user project—to support its developers, who operate as a nonprofit. NVivo and ATLAS.ti also have multimedia modules in addition to their Qualitative Data Analysis tools—however, the comprehensive package is prohibitively expensive for most small organizations. If you need to transcribe your audio or video content, keep in mind that tran¬scription services, even automated ones, can cost upward of $100 per hour of material.

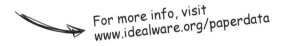

For more info, visit
www.idealware.org/paperdata

Custom Reporting Tools

While most *Case Management* or *Constituent Relationship Management* (CRM) systems will provide a range of flexible and useful reports, nonprofits looking to expand their report repertoire may want to consider designing their own reports using dedicated custom reporting tools. These reports can help with more complex evaluation efforts compared to built-in reports.

One solution would be to use a *Custom Reporting Tool* to augment your existing capabilities. Tools like Microsoft Access and Filemaker Pro are inexpensive, flexible options you may already be using. While these databases may be easier to use than other custom reporting tools, and can fairly easily import and export data to your constituent database, you'll need to create and maintain your own documentation so future staff members will be able to understand how the system works.

Crystal Reports from SAP is a widely-used custom reporting tool that provides the built-in reporting infrastructure for lots of software systems. However, the software is not the most user-friendly available, and while it's relatively inexpensive to start—about $500 for the license fee—there's a substantial jump in price to the more advanced versions. Crystal is still good for building basic forms and handling registration data, but for complex data analysis, it might be more than most nonprofits need or want. Other similar reporting tools include Birst and Logi Analytics from the business world, and Jaspersoft and BIRT, two open source solutions. You could also consider Microsoft's Reporting Services or Analysis Services, which come bundled with SQL server. ●

For more info, visit
www.idealware.org/customreports

Dashboards

Nonprofits track all sorts of information, from financial data to event attendance, volunteer participation, supporter involvement, and more. A *Dashboard*—sometimes called an Executive Dashboard—is simply a means of making it easier to understand and act on all this information by pulling it together in one place, with easy-to-understand visuals.

A good dashboard pulls together different, and sometimes disparate, metrics into a visually-appealing, easy-to-understand interface. Often it will show indicators that make it easy see progress against a goal—for example, a "traffic light" icon with a green, yellow, or red light to show whether fundraising revenue is proceeding according to plan.

Deciding what metrics to track and where to find that data can be deceptively challenging, as can the logistics behind creating and displaying it as a dashboard.

The simplest way to create a dashboard is to use one that already exists. Many *CRM* and *Donor Management* systems come with pre-programmed dashboards to track fundraising campaigns. For example, a flexible constituent database like Salesforce might track enough of the metrics you want to look at to simply create a dashboard as a report.

Microsoft SharePoint, often used as an Intranet and Portal solution, provides dashboard features for those willing to invest the time to learn and implement the software.

A more straightforward approach is to use Excel, as you can easily paste in updated figures, summarize them on a highly formatted summary tab, and use charts and automatic color-coding to create something highly readable—though it's more difficult to make it beautiful. You could do something similar with Google Drive. Though not quite as powerful for creating complex calculations, Google Drive does provide such graphic dashboard formats as a gauge to show where within a range your metric falls.

There's also business intelligence software, a whole class of tools designed to help you pull together data from different systems and transform it into easily readable reports and dashboards. This includes such tools as GoodData, iDashboards, Tableau, and other large software packages like the nonprofit-focused JCA Answers. These are more expensive systems to implement that make the most sense for larger organizations. Another option would be to use a *Custom Reporting Tool* like Crystal Reports or Jasper Reports to create a dashboard for your organization. These tools also have the advantage of flexible custom reports, which provide more information than would be otherwise available. ●

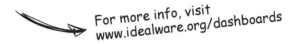

For more info, visit
www.idealware.org/dashboards

Maps and Geographical Information Systems (GIS)

Maps and Geographical Information Systems (GIS) allow nonprofits to display, analyze, and share data like addresses, ZIP codes, or latitude/longitude coordinates. By displaying information visually, maps can reveal significant data relationships that would otherwise be hard to notice. These tools range widely in complexity and in the features they offer.

It's critical to spend time understanding what information will be required, where you can get it, and the time it will take to transform it to a format that can be used by your (or any) GIS system. Pay close attention to ensure that your data is accurate—a misread GPS device or a misplaced decimal point can literally make a mountain out of a molehill. In addition to geographic data, you should also look to publicly available demographic information, like ethnicity or income level.

For many nonprofits, simply providing flat-map or globe views of the world, through what are often called "geobrowsers," will be enough to make sense of program data. These tools—like Google Maps and Google Earth, MapBuilder, and Virtual Earth 3D—are relatively simple to learn and use, allow you to plot data to create basic maps, and let you share your maps, but don't allow for in-depth data analysis. Google Drive's spreadsheet tool or BatchGeo can help you load a whole spreadsheet of addresses rather than plotting them one at a time.

Think about the type of data and how you want to visualize it before picking a tool. For example, Google Maps provides two-dimensional views, while Google Earth provides three-dimensional abilities to "fly" around your map, and adds abilities to raise and lower drawn shapes, potentially adding more data visualization possibilities. If you need to create thematic or "heat maps"—like displaying election results by district, for instance— you will likely need a more specialized tool. One of the few tools available that can create these types of maps is Microsoft MapPoint, available to nonprofits for $15 through TechSoup.

More sophisticated GIS packages allow you to work with data including imagery (such as maps), points (like a building), lines (such as streets), and polygons (areas enclosed by a shape, such as a census tract). You can then describe these points, lines, and polygons with other data, such as income levels, vacancy rates, or ethnicity. All of this data can be displayed on top of one another in layers on a map.

Sophisticated GIS allows more advanced understanding of all this data when layered together through functionality that includes queries and filters that help analysts focus in on particular data and layers; functions for thinning and generalizing data; tools for reconciling physical features from two different data layers into the same view; and more. Advanced tools like MapWindow, Manifold GIS, or the industry-leader Esri ArcGIS require strong data-analysis skills, and using these tools effectively can require quite a leap in expertise from the basic mapping systems. ●

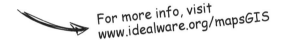

For more info, visit
www.idealware.org/mapsGIS

Measuring Social Media

Once you start using social media, how do you know if your efforts are working? There are many tools and options for measuring your success, from simple general approaches to tool-specific solutions.

You can use a search engine, like Google, Bing, or others, to provide a count of how often your name is popping up online, and for a bit more flexibility, Google Alerts will email you online mentions of keywords— for example, your organization's name. In addition to tracking your website, most *Web Analytics* software can help you better under-stand your blog activity and monitor traffic to your website from all your social media channels.

Most social media channels offer some built-in or third-party way to analyze your activity. Facebook Insights is a reasonably powerful tool available to any organization whose page has at least 30 fans, and platforms like HootSuite provide basic metrics for Twitter. And most blogs can be effectively measured with a combination of the blogging site's built-in metrics, FeedBurner, and web analytics.

For more streamlined or automated monitoring, aggregating tools help keep an eye on multiple aspects of your social media efforts. Tools like Social Mention and NutshellMail aggregate mentions of keywords or your brand across multiple social media channels, while SproutSocial, RowFeeder and Kurrently can create reports based on Twitter and Facebook.

There are also measurement tools specific to each social media channel. Klout measures your Twitter influence, Booshaka measures Facebook fan interactions, and quintly collects general Facebook page data and calculates change rates and other complicated statistics.

For larger organizations, mid-level tools like Small Act's Thrive and Spredfast offer fairly comprehensive pictures of your social media activities. At the higher-end of the price scale are Radian6 (now part of the Salesforce Marketing Cloud) and Lithium, which measure influ-ence, deliver comparisons to competitors and data on your market share, and provide tangible methods of improving. Both platforms offer nonprofit discounts. ●

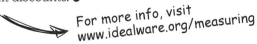

For more info, visit
www.idealware.org/measuring

Online Listening

Online Listening Tools help nonprofits "hear" what people are saying about their causes or organizations online. Whether they're saying good things about your programs or questioning your methods, knowing what they're saying and who's doing the talking can help you fine-tune your plans, consider future actions, and prepare appropriate responses.

A number of *Online Listening Tools* require you to actively search. You type in a keyword, such as your organization or executive director's name, to find online discussions, conversations, or mentions. Different tools are distinguished more by what online areas they search—for example, the entire web, a specific *Social Networking Site,* or *Blogs*—rather than what methods they use.

For instance, Google searches the entire web while Google Blog Search lets you also target blogs specifically. Technorati searches blog posts. BoardTracker searches discussion boards by both thread and tags.

Similarly, you can search for topics in *Facebook, Twitter,* Google+, YouTube and Flickr, among others, by using each site's respective search functions.

The most robust way to handle online listening is to use an *RSS* tool to create a "listening dashboard." Most of the sites above let you create *RSS* feeds for particular keywords—you can then pull those feeds together into a "Dashboard" using an *RSS* reader. This method often results in a huge amount of duplicate content, but advanced tools like Yahoo! Pipes can help reduce the clutter.

Higher-end tools like Radian6 (now part of the Salesforce Marketing Cloud) and Jive can create robust listening dashboards with less work, but they're best suited for organizations with the resources to afford them and enough online mentions to make it worthwhile. Don't forget the more traditional ways to listen to people, like *Online Surveys,* phone calls, or old fashioned feet-on-the-ground conversations with people in your community. ●

For more info, visit
www.idealware.org/listening

Consider a Clipping Service

Clipping Services, or Media Monitoring Services, can monitor social media as well as online news outlets and print media. Most offer software so organizations can track these sources themselves, but others can do the tracking for you and deliver reports on the results. Tools in this area include Sprout Social, uberVU, and Actionly at the low-end of the price range. At higher tiers, there is Trackur, Thrive, and CustomScoop, which can cost hundreds or even thousands of dollars per month. These tools allow you to keep track of social media followers, note when media outlets promote your resources, or look at the ratio of positive-to-negative press about your organization.

Online Surveys

Online Surveys are a cost-effective way to deliver surveys, collect results, and possibly even analyze the data—all through one central package. These tools let you easily define survey questions and possible responses using an online interface, send constituents links to take the survey, and download response data. Basic survey features are available through some other types of systems, like *Integrated Online Systems, Broadcast Email Tools,* or such online form builders as Google Forms, Wufoo, or Formstack, but a number of dedicated tools are available.

Some, like SurveyMonkey, SurveyGizmo, and Polldaddy, offer free options with limited functionality, or a surprisingly robust set of features for $200-$2,000 per year. These types of tools tend to provide considerable support for different types of survey questions, but typically only limited ability to analyze the results. Some of them even let you embed a form in your website rather than redirect people to an external site.

If you want to conduct larger-scale research projects, a more powerful survey package like Qualtrics, QuestionPro, or Key Survey might be a better fit. These tools support more advanced question formats, survey logic and sophisticated data analysis starting at several thousand dollars per year. LimeSurvey, a free and open source tool, provides similarly advanced functionality. The more complex feature-set makes this whole class of tool more difficult to use without training—especially for those without prior survey-design expertise. ●

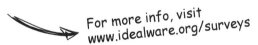
For more info, visit
www.idealware.org/surveys

Want to Just Ask a Few Quick Questions?

If these tools seem like overkill for your needs, consider Google Form functionality, which lets you easily create and post a form online for free. The Summary Report feature provides a helpful executive report of data and submissions, too. Polldaddy offers similar features to integrate a small poll into your website.

Program Evaluation

Articles, conferences and books have been devoted to the concept and strategies behind evaluating the success of programs, but there's no single software specific to the practice. *Program Evaluation* is not primarily a technology issue—software can help you track and analyze the data you'll need, but in order to make any meaningful conclusions, you need to first carefully identify your evaluation strategy.

Consider how complex your data needs are. Can you easily track everything you need about each point of data in a spreadsheet row? If so, don't shy away from a simple Microsoft Excel or online Google Drive spreadsheet.

Many nonprofits track much of their data at a client level and then roll it up across multiple clients to help them better understand the broader impacts of their programs. If the data you need for your evaluation plan is tracked at a person level, a *Case Management System, Constituent Relationship Management System* or some other kind of constituent database is likely to be the best way to manage and report on it.

If you're tracking things that aren't specifically related to particular constituents—for example, water quality over time, or the outcomes of 30 different programs conducted by 30 different organizations—start by checking to see if you're using any other systems that track information at the same level. If you're already tracking information on the 30 programs (in a grants management system, for instance), you can likely also store and report on the outcomes of those programs in that same system.

But if other options fail, you may need to use a database platform to build your own system. Consider Microsoft Access or File-Maker Pro, which give you a base set of tools on which to build systems to enter and report on data, or a *Constituent Relationship Management* platform like Salesforce or Microsoft Dynamics CRM. These platforms will let you track and interrelate both constituent and non-constituent metrics in the same system.

There are also tools geared toward helping you understand what your data means. *Charts and Diagrams* and *MAPS and GIS* tools can help you to visualize your data, while *Dashboard* tools can provide summarized views. If you're looking to provide statistical evidence of efficacy, you'll need *Statistical Analysis Tools* to analyze quantitative data about your programs. ●

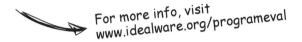
For more info, visit www.idealware.org/programeval

RSS

RSS, or *Really Simple Syndication,* is an easy way to stay on top of information you're interested in reading. Instead of visiting a number of blogs and websites every day, you subscribe to sites via *RSS* and their updates are sent to you.

If a *Blog* or website supports *RSS,* it typically displays an orange *RSS* icon somewhere on the page or in the navigation bar. You can then subscribe to the RSS feed by simply clicking on that icon.

To view the feeds you subscribe to, you'll need some kind of software package that's designed to pull in and display feeds. Many internet or email browsers—like Internet Explorer, Firefox, or Microsoft Outlook—include functionality that allows you to easily see feeds in one place.

If you want to follow a lot of different feeds, more specialized tools can help. The loss of the popular Google Reader tool was a blow to *RSS* fans, but there are still options available. These tools, called "feed readers," "news readers," "blog readers," or "*RSS* aggregators," let you see and manage all the *RSS* feeds you've subscribed to. Feed readers can be web-based, like Feedly, or desktop-based like NewsGator's FeedDemon for PCs and Vienna for Macs. Most are free and make it easy to see and organize updates for all the sites you've subscribed to. Other tools, like FeedBlitz, let you subscribe to *RSS* through email (instead of a feed reader).

You can also use readers in conjunction with *Online Listening* to monitor what people are saying about your organization. ●

For more info, visit
www.idealware.org/rss

Use RSS to Spread Information

Keep **RSS** in mind as you build your own website and **Blog.**
Some people follow online information solely by **RSS**, so make
sure you offer the ability to subscribe. Most **Blog** tools and
Web Content Management Systems support **RSS** feeds.
Alternatively, tools like WebRSS and RapidFeeds can help you
create RSS feeds from any type of content with a little effort.
Google FeedBurner can provide information about how many
people are subscribed and viewing your content via **RSS.**

Statistical Analysis Tools

Not all analysis can be easily accomplished through reports. If your organization needs to find trends in survey data (like feedback from constituents who have gone through your programs) or large datasets (like U.S. Census or demographic information about your service area), *Statistical Analysis* software can help. While such technology can be inexpensive to start, the more feature-rich options can cost upward of $6,000 for a single license. Statistics is also not something you can pick up easily, either; these packages can require a considerable investment in staff time and training.

If your software budget is tight and your statistical analysis needs are basic, you might consider using Microsoft Excel. While normally thought of as a *Spreadsheet* tool, Excel can handle most statistical needs, and you probably already have it. If not, it's relatively inexpensive at about $120 as a standalone product, and nonprofits can obtain a license for the office from TechSoup at great discount. But Excel isn't an optimal solution— it can't automatically handle missing cell values, for instance. Many of these limitations can be overcome through free add-ons, like the Analysis Toolpak for Windows or Statplus: Mac LE for Mac OS.

While Excel is good for most of the basic analysis you'll need, it won't take long to outgrow it. A widely used and well-respected option is R. R is an open source solution, meaning it's free to acquire, but requires some technical savvy to use, as there is no graphical user interface. Instead, all functions are entered through the command-line. R runs on a variety of operating systems, and its thriving user community will help if you get stuck. Nonprofit staffers familiar with programming basics and with a firm grasp of statistical concepts may find R a good choice.

For users with moderate-sized datasets, Stata is an affordable option, starting at about $1,000 for STATA/IC, the standard version. Less technical users will likely appreciate Stata's menu-based graphical interface, but there is a command-line interface for those with more programming know-how. Stata is easily customized, and draws praise for its tech support, helpful user community, and relative ease of use. However, the software lacks the power of some other options on the market—for example, Stata can only open one dataset at a time.

IBM's answer to statistical analysis, SPSS Statistics, has a point-and-click graphical interface that doesn't require substantial programming knowledge. This ease of use comes at the expense of some control over statistical output. Nonprofits in need of basic statistical analysis won't find this an issue, but if you seek to do more sophisticated data manipulation, SPSS might prove frustrating. And it's relatively expensive—about $6,000 for a license.

If you've got substantial data analysis needs, you might need an enterprise-level system. With more than one-third of the market share, SAS is the giant of the statistical analysis software scene. Strengths include power and efficiency in linking large data sets, and a comprehensive built-in set of statistical analysis features. SAS Analytics Pro, the entry-level desktop version of the software, costs around $8,500 per user for first-year license fees alone and about $2,000 per year for ongoing use. This software is not for novices, and requires a high degree of statistical and technological expertise to run it. However, SAS offers excellent tech support, and its prevalence means it will likely be easier to find other organizations in your network that also use the software than other tools. ●

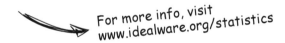
For more info, visit www.idealware.org/statistics

Web Analytics

Web Analytics software tracks your site's statistics—visitors to each page, what sites they came from, who they are, and more—to help you understand and improve your website and readership. You may already have some of the tools you need. It's possible that the vendor you pay to host your website offers you access to some web statistics through the same control panel you use to administer email addresses, check available file space, and manage permissions. These tools (AWStats and The Webalizer are common packages) offer basic reports with little in-depth analysis, but are a free, convenient way to get your feet wet with analytics.

Google Analytics is widely considered the dominant player in this space. It's free and widely used, and dramatically more powerful than any other free option. Getting started requires access to your website's HTML code, and at least a few hours of work—and more to track documents like PDFs or Flash content. You'll be able to see sophisticated metrics, analyze data across timeframes or pages, and set up the "traffic reports" you'd like to see. The powerful interface may overwhelm less tech-savvy users, but there are lots of books,trainings, and free YouTube tutorials available.

A number of high-end analytics tools, like ClickTracks, Webtrends, and Omniture, are particularly useful to track traffic behind a password barrier, or on sites with sophisticated multimedia content (which Google Analytics can't easily track). They also provide technical support, which Google Analytics does not. Prices vary, starting as low as $25 per month and ranging way up to $1,000 per month or more. ●

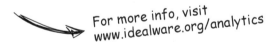

For more info, visit
www.idealware.org/analytics

Almost every nonprofit needs to coordinate the work of multiple people, from staff to volunteers to board members. Collaboration software can help you share information, hold conversations and manage projects—whether your teammates are in your office or around the world.

All of the software names highlighted within the text are covered in more detail in this guide. Most of them are included in this section, and follow immediately after the descriptions. If you're interested in a software type and can't find it in this section, you can look it up in the Index.

Even if you're a single-person organization, chances are you don't work alone—these tools can help you collaborate with colleagues, board members, volunteers, and consultants.

....

Strongly Consider...

If your staff or team members are spread out geographically, or if you regularly meet with constituents, volunteers, or others, *Online Conferencing* can provide an easy way to facilitate meetings without the overhead and logistics of travel or accommodations. It can also make it possible to host trainings, Q&A's, and another events.

Keeping Ahead of the Curve...

If you work with multiple people on multiple tasks and deadlines, *Project Management Software* can make it easier to keep responsibilities and accomplishments straight and help people understand their roles in the grander scheme.

For tasks in which you want to share information but not documents, *Collaborative Documents* might be a better fit for your needs—they allow multiple people to work on a single document at the same time. *Screencasting* and *Screenshots* can also help with online trainings by creating images of your computer screen—or video recordings of your actions on the screen—to pass along to others by email or over the web. *Screenshots* can show how software looks, or is supposed to look, while *Screencasts* can teach others how to perform certain actions.

On the Cutting Edge...

eLearning takes online training to the next level. With the right tools, you can create instruction modules rich with multimedia content to instruct students in an out-of-the-classroom setting. Such lessons used to require specialized course developers to design and create, but now they're within reach of anyone with the right tool and a good plan. *Learning Management Systems* are another option for organizations that offer full-fledged courses or need to manage training.

With *Online Chat,* people can type questions a website to communicate with an audience—say, your organization hosts a Q and A with an expert, and constituents can log on and see the questions and answers the moment they're typed, or ask their own.

If your organization wants to collaborate on content to a greater extent than collaborative docs support, a *Wiki* might be the answer. *Wikis* are user-editable websites that serve as a comprehensive, easy way for a large group of users—like staff or constituents—to create and share a growing pool of information.

Finally, *Board Support Software* is growing in popularity in the nonprofit sector. This cohesive collection of tools and materials enables members of an organization's Board of Directors to access, print, and comment on board documents, take notes, and communicate among each other and with staff, keeping board members informed and engaged. ●

Board Support Software

Board portals are designed specifically to help members of organization's boards of directors fulfill their roles and collaborate effectively despite being spread out geographically. Regulations in the for-profit sector that put stringent new requirements on board information and management led to the rise of this software, which means it is first and foremost secure. But in the past few years, as prices have come down and interest from the nonprofit sector has grown, vendors have adapted their offerings to better meet the needs of nonprofit boards. However, the tools remain reasonably expensive, and more within the reach of larger organizations than small ones.

Portals from BoardVantage, BoardWorks, Diligent Boardbooks, BoardEffect, Directors Desk, and Thomson BoardLink all offer varied functionality, but many overlapping features.

Portals typically include tools to create a board book—the package of documents to be reviewed at a particular meeting—and centrally manage organizational documents, as well as the ability to broadcast materials to all board members, to a specific committee or to selected individuals. Board members usually have defined access to materials, with user-level access to allow support staff to see appropriate materials without access to confidential sections of the portal. They can take notes online as they review meeting packets, and access these notes during meetings.

Other typical functionality includes on- and off-line accessibility that lets board members access materials over the web and download them for review while offline, such as when traveling, still ensuring the same strict security.

Most packages provide calendaring functions, and can link calendars to materials for scheduled meetings, as well as e-mail and discussion tools with confidentiality controls that limit access to appropriate staff. Some also include survey tools for polling board members or conducting board assessments, and let board chairs call for online voting, when appropriate. ●

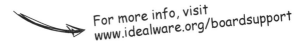

For more info, visit
www.idealware.org/boardsupport

Collaborative Documents

If you've ever emailed a document to a group of people for comments—and then tried to revise the original with all their edits—you can appreciate the value of collaborating online. Each person can update the original document, and everyone with permission can view the changes in real time.

Collaborative Document tools tend to be inexpensive and easy to use. Google Drive is the best known example. It lets you work with an unlimited set of users on text documents, spreadsheets, presentations, or diagrams, and you can invite them by email or set the document so that anyone with the link can log in. (Users need a Google account to edit, but they're free and easy to create.) There's a helpful interface for users to manage the documents they can access, and you can manage permissions through Google Groups..

If you need more sophisticated formatting and features than Google Drive offers, Zoho, and ThinkFree provide more-robust feature-sets for about $50 per user, per year.

Alternatively, many online *Project Management Software* packages like Basecamp or Central Desktop's SocialBridge offer means to work together on documents or spreadsheets; if your group plans to work together over time, and to manage tasks, view shared calendars, or share files online, a single tool that manages all these functions may make more sense.

To collaborate on a complex document, particularly one with a lot of different sections—like a set of manuals or a book—a *Wiki* lets multiple people edit existing documents as well as create new pages or sections. It's a collaborative website, not just a collaborative document, which provides more power to manage a great deal of content, but will also have a higher learning curve for collaborators. Once content is finalized, it can be downloaded in various file formats. ●

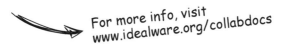
For more info, visit www.idealware.org/collabdocs

COLLABORATIVE DOCUMENTS

eLearning

Want to teach staff or constituents over the web, or produce online classes? *eLearning* is an umbrella term for any instructional method that uses technology in place of a classroom, but typically refers to multimedia modules that teach students using recorded interactive lessons accessed on-demand. *Online Conferencing* tools provide the ability to deliver a live online presentation, and often to record it, but *eLearning* tools can typically provide more sophisticated on-demand courses, particularly useful for training a large volume of people who aren't all in the same location.

Screencasting tools are a lightweight way to create an on-demand interactive module, but many more-robust tools are available.

Simple *eLearning* modules can include a few pages of text, with buttons to advance the pages and a short multiple-choice quiz to test for comprehension. More complex modules can include animation and immersive content, like teaching users a schematic and then quizzing them on its parts, or use branching logic to provide different course content based on how the student answers certain questions.

Tools like CourseLab, Adobe Captivate, Articulate, Lectora, ToolBook, and SmartBuilder help develop the content and the interface with which students interact. These software packages will guide you through the creation of core elements like text, graphics, and narration, and help add such embellishments as animation and interactivity that can engage learners and enhance the overall experience.

eLearning modules are often offered through *Learning Management Systems* (LMS), like Moodle, Blackboard, or other systems that offer both an LMS and a module creator. These systems help guide students through multiple modules and form learning communities. Modules can also be delivered in other common formats like HTML pages, Flash files, or CD-ROM packages for kiosk use. ●

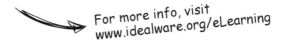

For more info, visit
www.idealware.org/eLearning

File Sharing

Whether your colleagues are in the same room or on another continent, you likely need a way to create and edit documents as a team. There are far better ways than just emailing attachments back and forth.

If you want to share files with people in the same office, a computer that serves as a "file server" is a typical solution. A file server is simply a computer that acts as the primary place that staff can store and access their files. The server is then connected to the organization's other computers, via a network.

For those who are in different geographic locations, *Collaborative Documents* such as the free Google Drive let users share documents over the web and internally for a short-term collaboration between a limited number of users. All changes are saved and appear instantly to other users, avoiding the confusion that can come from passing around multiple versions of files.

Tools like Dropbox, SugarSync, and Microsoft SkyDrive provide basic functionality to allow users to synchronize files on their computer with those on other machines. When the shared files are updated on one computer, the files are automatically synchronized on all other machines over the internet, regardless of where each computer is.

Egnyte and Box (formerly Box.net) go beyond the basic to provide online enterprise-class replacements for traditional hardware file servers. These solutions provide centrally managed user permissions to allow organizations control over who can access which file and to track access and changes to data via audit logs.

Alternatively, Microsoft's SharePoint provides organizations with project websites that include the ability to let users upload files, "check out" documents so others can't edit them at the same time, and share contact information. SharePoint Online provides this functionality over the internet, while SharePoint Foundation 2010 provides an installed version. Or you could use a hardware solution like a Virtual Private Network (VPN) to create a secure way for remote users to access your entire network.

To share unformatted information with a larger group, consider a *Wiki*, a website where users collaboratively edit a document using their browsers. *Intranets and Portals* often offer file-sharing capabilities, as well.

For very complex operations, enterprise-level *Document Management Systems* let users track document updates, store previous versions, check out documents to prevent simultaneous editing, and rigorously manage and search documents. ●

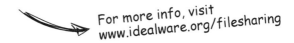

For more info, visit
www.idealware.org/filesharing

Intranets and Portals

In addition to their external websites, many organizations have secure sites accessible only by staff. These internal sites, called *Intranets or Portals,* are widespread in the business world, and are becoming increasingly common among nonprofits. (The word "portal" implies a somewhat more sophisticated site that brings diverse information together, but for the most part, it's synonymous with an intranet.)

Sites used to share confidential organizational information, documents, reference materials and other resources, intranets can be built a number of different ways—including using the same *Content Management System* as your public website, or another one. You could also use a *Wiki,* which lets you create a relatively open and collaborative site that can be updated by staff.

Internal-facing social networking applications like Yammer can also let your staff quickly share status with each other—essentially, they're internal tools that work similarly to *Twitter.* For those using the Salesforce CRM platform, its Chatter functionality has similar features.

Or you could create an organization-wide "start page" using an application like Google Sites or Netvibes for Enterprise. These tools let you add "widgets," or small blocks of information, that provide announcements, links, or information. Each individual user can then customize their homepage to add things like news feeds or weather reports.

As another option, tools like Liferay and Microsoft SharePoint provide a range of templates and features for document sharing, task lists, calendars, search functions, and *Blogs* and *Wikis.* If your intranet will support hundreds or thousands of documents, a *Document Management System* might be a better fit than lighter-weight solutions.

Whatever tool you use, keep in mind that an effective intranet is as much a matter of staff training and culture change as it is a technical one. It's relatively easy to publish information for your staff; it's considerably harder to help them find it, use it and keep it up to date. ●

For more info, visit www.idealware.org/intranets

Learning Management Systems

Learning Management Systems (LMS) help organizations that conduct trainings or other educational programs organize curriculum-related materials, forums, grades, submission of class materials, and other online communications. Some systems also offer *eLearning* modules that allow courses to be streamed over the web.

Learning Management Systems sometimes offer the ability to conduct standardized tests, or you might choose to outsource this to an outside company like Scantron. Such tests are available in paper or electronic forms, and external providers will analyze and score results for a fee—or let you do the analysis yourself.

Popular LMS products include the open source Moodle, which allows for grading, online discussion forums and message boards, messaging and other teacher-student interactions, and some file delivery, but not synchronous online meetings. As an open source project, there's a variety of custom reports available on the Moodle platform that could help with program evaluation, and you can write your own in SQL. Another well-known open source LMS is Sakai, developed by a consortium of universities including the University of Michigan, MIT, and Stanford and adopted and customized by many higher education institutions. Sakai also runs on SQL-based queries for custom reports. There's also the proprietary Blackboard suite of products, which includes Learn and Collaborate for Learning Management Systems, and Analytics for statistics and reporting. ●

For more info, visit
www.idealware.org/elearning

Online Chat

Similar to instant messaging, online chat tools let people type messages into a website to communicate with an audience. The audience might be an entire group of people logged in to the discussion, or two people chatting directly. *Online Chat* tools help organizations hold live online exchanges (like "chat with a celebrity" or "ask the expert" sessions), offer online client services with real-time responses, host a forum for comments during a live conference session, and more.

A number of free, straightforward tools support this, including CoveritLive, which lets you create a live, moderated group chat functionality on your own website. Another, Campfire, supports internal group chats, but can be adapted for public chat on your website. The more robust LivePerson allows real-time chat on your site, geared toward customer services. ●

For more info, visit
www.idealware.org/chat

Consider Twitter

Some organizations are using **Twitter** for online chats—especially to encourage comments via laptop or text messaging during a live conference. If you ask people to include a "hashtag" (simply a # sign followed by a keyword, like #DogLovers12) in their Twitter posts, it's relatively easy to group all resulting posts together for display via an LCD projector at the event or on your website.

Online Conferencing

Technology has made it possible for the workforce to spread out geographically, but email and phone calls only go so far facilitating communication. Sometimes you need visuals to illustrate a conversation. Whether you want your audience all to see the same slides or document over the web, display your computer screen for a demo, or conduct more formal online seminars (often called webinars), *Online Conferencing* tools can help.

If all you need is the ability to do a video conference, Skype, ooVoo, and Google+ Hangouts offer useful and free audio and video conferencing for those who have a computer headset or speakers and microphone and a webcam, and Skype and Google+ Hangouts now have the capability to share your screen as well. WebHuddle and Yugma also provide features to share your screen and take comments by chat, and are priced attractively. WebHuddle is currently free during its beta period, and Yugma costs between $26 and $1,600 per year based on the size of your group. Audio and screen-sharing quality with these tools can vary, however, and they can be less reliable than the more expensive tools below.

If you need to share your desktop or an application with your conference participants, there are a number of low-cost tools available, like Screen Stream and Join.me at the lower end of the price scale, or TeamViewer and Glance for organizations willing to spend a couple hundred dollars on a tool. Screen Stream is available for free, and Join.me has a free version for up to 10 participants—for up to 250 participants, Join.me Pro starts at $149 per year. Glance starts at $500 per year, and TeamViewer starts at $750 for up to 15 participants and unlimited hosts. UberConference is another affordable option.

Tools like GoToMeeting, GoToWebinar, WebEx, Adobe Connect, and ReadyTalk cost more, but are more widely relied on and dependable. They often provide such features as integrated audio and visual recordings, integrated toll-free conference-calling lines, and other advanced interactive tools. Cost is often complicated to determine, as it's based on the features you want and the number of people in your meetings. It generally ranges from $200 to $5,000 per year. ●

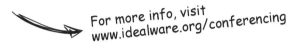

For more info, visit
www.idealware.org/conferencing

Check on Audio Conferencing!

Note that the posted prices for these tools often does not include the cost of audio conferencing via a phone line. Some tools provide Voice Over IP (VOIP), which provides free audio over the internet, but that requires that all participants have computer speakers, as well as some technical know-how. Otherwise you'll need a telephone conferencing line. Online conferencing vendors will generally provide one – often at extra cost--or you can use a service like FreeConferenceCall.com. Note that FreeConferenceCall.com is free for you, but your participants must pay for their own long-distance services.

Project Management

Managing projects can be confusing, especially with multiple team members—potentially in different locations—who need to coordinate tasks, documents, and deadlines. There are a number of different types of tools that will handle a few pieces of this management puzzle, but unfortunately there's no such thing as a one-size-fits-all *Project Management* tool.

To create an overall project plan, with tasks, dependencies, time estimates, and resource allocation, consider tools like OmniPlan or Microsoft Project. Microsoft Project, while popular and powerful, is complex and may be overkill for the majority of nonprofit projects.

Document sharing is another frequently mentioned project management feature. See File Sharing for various options to share files across a team.

Organizations that need to track complex tasks—for instance, those that include conversations, priorities, attachments, or software development issues—often use separate issue-tracking software like JIRA, DoneDone, and Unfuddle. These tools are typically available for a small fee, from $10 to $100 per year.

There are also some useful free and open-source issue-tracking software systems that could be used for complex task lists, including Mantis, Bugzilla, and Trac. You'll need to install these systems on your own web server, and maintain those servers yourself, which makes them a better solution for more technical organizations. Many companies use commercially hosted versions of these systems to eliminate the risk of tracking issues on the same server that runs their sites.

Many project managers would like a single system that handles all of these things. Unfortunately, there's no tool likely to include all the functionality of each of the sophisticated, specialized tools. However, a number of general project management tools like Basecamp, Central Desktop's SocialBridge, OpenAtrium, Zoho, DreamTeam for Salesforce, or Goplan incorporate basic project planning, document sharing, task management, shared calendars and online discussion boards. These web-based tools are particularly useful for geographically diverse teams, or for teams that include members from outside your organization. ●

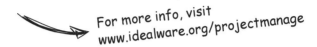

For more info, visit
www.idealware.org/projectmanage

What About Time Tracking Tools?

You may also want to explore lightweight, cloud-based time tracking systems like Toggl or RescueTime for hour-by-hour breakdowns of how your team is spending its time on projects. This data is useful for planning out how much time future projects will take, as well as for identifying areas where staff time can be saved. These systems vary in sophistication of the data you can extract, but many have low-cost subscription plans that offer more features.

Screenshots and Screencasting

Sometimes it's more useful to show a group what you're talking about rather than just tell them. *Screenshot* tools let you do just that by capturing an image of your screen that you can share with others—typically in .JPG or .PNG format. Similarly, *Screencasting* tools let you actually record or make a movie of what's happening on your screen. (If you want to share your screen in real time rather than as a recording, *Online Conferencing* software might be more useful.)

Most computers let you capture a simple screen image without additional tools. Both Windows and Apple computers allow you to capture the screen through keyboard shortcuts (Alt + Print Screen on Windows, Apple key + Shift + 3 or + 4 on a Mac). For more functionality, Windows computers with version 7 and 8 come with a "Snipping Tool" that allows you to both capture and edit screenshots. Lightscreen, a free download, is similar to the Snipping Tool, but includes such additional features as delayed captures. Screenium is a popular tool for Mac users.

Screenshots can be embedded in creative ways in PowerPoint presentations, blogs, and websites, or used for trainings and product demonstrations. If you rely heavily on screenshots, look for a tool with more powerful options. PicPick is a tool with many options both for screen captures and for editing. TechSmith's Snagit or Easy Screen Capture are geared toward the professional. These tools are all under $50 and provide better control over selection areas—including scrolling screens and odd shapes—and let you apply effects like borders and drop shadows, highlight sections of the screen with arrows, or shade out unwanted areas. You could also look to documentation building tools, like Screen-Steps from Blue Mango Learning Systems, which offer more features than regular screenshot tools for organizations building trainings.

Free browser add-ons offer more screen capture facility than is built in to Windows, but not as much as the commercial products. FireShot works for Firefox, and Screen Capture works for Google's Chrome. Because they are browser based, they function across platforms and will work on Windows, Mac or Linux machines.

Screencasts that walk users through a particular task, complete with voiceover, are helpful for online trainings or demonstrations. TechSmith's Jing offers easy to use, stripped down features in both its free version and inexpensive Pro version. The more expensive TechSmith's Camtasia and Adobe Captivate offer more power to edit video and synch it with audio. Camtasia offers features to pan and zoom around your screencast, while Captivate excels at adding interactivity.

None of these tools is particularly sophisticated in terms of video editing or interactive elements, however. *Video Editing Software* provides more flexibility for complex editing, and higher-end *eLearning* software offers more opportunities for animations and for viewer involvement. ●

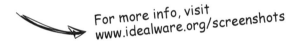
For more info, visit
www.idealware.org/screenshots

Wikis

A *Wiki* is a web page whose content can be modified by multiple people. Administrators manage specifically who can see and edit sections or pages. *Wikis* are great for creating content collaboratively—they can be accessed online from anywhere, they let multiple people edit simultaneously, and prior versions are automatically saved and easily restored.

However, many *Wikis* feel fairly technical to update. For instance, staff members may need to learn and use formatting tags—for example, [h1] to denote that a header should be large and bold. These tags aren't particularly complicated, but can be intimidating to less-technical users.

Those looking to get started quickly will benefit from hosted *Wiki* software, which you can access over the web. Wikispacesand PBworks offer free, basic hosted services, but taking advantage of all available features can cost $1,000 per year or more. Wikispaces and Zoho's wiki tool allow for easy formatting without the use of tags.

If your organization is comfortable downloading and installing software on your own web server, there are a number of free and open source options, like MediaWiki (originally developed for Wikipedia), DokuWiki, and Tiki Wiki. Confluence, typically a fee-based product, also offers free licenses to nonprofits. ●

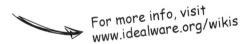

For more info, visit
www.idealware.org/wikis

The Many Uses of Wikis

Wikis can be useful for creating or sharing information among a group—for example, as a collaborative website like Wikipedia, for project management or document development, to share best practices, or as an **Intranet or Portal.** If your constituents are spread out across the country or the globe, a wiki lets people keep pertinent data up-to-date in a central, easily accessible location.

You have constituents: donors, event attendees, volunteers, board members, and more. You need a system to track them and to store all the information you'll need to build your relationship.

What type of system will best help you depends on your specific needs. This section will help you think about what exists, and what might work best for you.

All of the software names highlighted within the text are covered in more detail in this guide. Most of them are included in this section, and follow immediately after the descriptions. If you're interested in a software type and can't find it in this section, you can look it up in the Index.

Every organization needs some way to track donors, event attendees, volunteers, and other constituents, but which system type you choose requires some consideration. The different types of constituent management software available range widely in cost and features. When choosing, you need to carefully weigh the type of information that's most important to you, as well as how you plan to access and use that information.

· ·

The system types include:

- *Constituent Relationship Management (CRM).* These systems are designed to track comprehensive data about each constituent—not only the donations and membership dues, but also, potentially, event attendance, volunteer work, and anything else you might care to track about a particular individual. These systems are not designed to specialize in any one specific function. Instead, they're typically flexible to let you tailor them to the processes you need to support. If constituents have complicated relationships with your organization, or tend to cross organizational boundaries—for example, program alumni often become donors—a CRM can be a useful way to get a full picture of each constituent. Some people use "CRM" as a catchall term for any constituent database, but at Idealware, we use it to describe this specific kind of flexible system that has substantial integration with your organization's online presence.

- *Donor Management.* These systems provide targeted support to track donors, prospects, pledges, premiums and giving levels, matching gifts, and sometimes grants and corporate sponsorships. Some provide support for additional constituents, like event attendees, volunteers, or members. However, these systems are best suited for organizations that hold individual fundraising as a top priority.

- *Integrated Online Systems.* These types of systems combine different online functions in a single package. For example, they'll often let you track donors and other constituents, send broadcast emails, take online donations and event registrations, and even manage a website, all in one system. It can save you a lot of time and hassle to have all this data in one place, but make sure your other needs are also met—these online specialty tools often aren't as strong at helping with direct mail processes and donor list-generation tasks as Donor Management Systems. To take full advantage of these tools, small organizations typically use them to replace any existing constituent databases.

- *Association Management Software.* Generally synonymous with membership management, these systems track organizations and individuals as members. They tend to be strong at managing yearly dues, events, and online member interactions. More advanced systems often also provide substantial donor management support, as well as functions like Broadcast Email and Online Payments.

- *Case Management Software.* Case management systems will track the information you need to work with a client, such as address, job history, medical history, and child care situation. They'll also track communications between your staff and the client, the individualized plan for your client, and the progress toward the plan, and let you report on all the information you've collected and maybe go so far as to support overall program evaluation.

- *Volunteer Management Software.* Do you work with a lot of volunteers, and track their hours, interests, schedules, and contributions? If so, a system that can help with those tasks could be useful—it could even help you recruit people and collect information about potential volunteers online.

- *Specialized and Custom Constituent Tracking Systems.* Though many nonprofits are well-served by constituent databases that aren't designed for their specific type of organizations, others have complex requirements that can be best supported by software designed to meet them. From religious organizations to legal aid firms, we'll talk through a few of these areas—and when, if ever, it makes sense to use a custom-built solution.

In practice, these types of software aren't as distinct as they might seem. For instance, some systems offer a lot of support for donor management, the ability to track members and volunteers, considerable flexibility to track other constituents, and some support for *Broadcast Email* and *Online Donations*. Are they Donor, Member, Volunteer, Integrated Online, or CRM systems? It doesn't matter, as long as they meet your needs. ●

Association Management Software

Do you want to track your organizational members, dues schedules, member benefits, invitations to events and workshops, or other relevant data? You might find an *Association Management* system useful. Generally synonymous with membership management, association management tends to imply a larger system that tracks organizations and individuals as members.

At the lower end of the spectrum, less-expensive online tools like Wild Apricot, 123Signup, MemberClicks, YourMembership.com, and Tendenci are likely to work best for associations with less complicated membership and benefit structures. They range from about $25 to $400 per month, depending on tools and how many members you're tracking.

In general, solutions with mid-range pricing (typically, between $3,000 and $15,000 per year) offer deeper functionality and greater ability to configure the application to meet individual associations' needs. Hosted solutions—like i4a's Association Management System, JL Systems' NOAH, and Avectra's netFORUM—tend to provide lower startup cost and implementation time, but are somewhat less flexible. If you need more flexibility, consider solutions that provide both the systems and the consulting necessary to tailor them to your needs, like Euclid ClearVantage.

At the high end of the market, systems like Advanced Solutions International's iMIS, GoMembers, TCS Software Prevail, Aptify, and Personify/TIMSS target larger professional or trade associations that have the technical staff in place to adopt and sustain enterprise software. They offer complex features, customized toolsets and stronger vendor support partnerships. In addition, higher-end systems are designed to manage large conferences and provide advanced tools for communicating with members. Pricing for the software alone ranges from $15,000 to more than $100,000 in annual costs, and implementation generally ranges from $30,000 up into the hundreds of thousands of dollars. ●

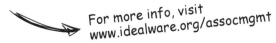 For more info, visit www.idealware.org/assocmgmt

Case Management Software

Case Management systems—sometimes called client management systems—will track the information you need to work with a client, such as their age, address, job history, medical history, and child care situation. They'll also track communications between your staff and the client, the individualized plan for your client, and the progress toward the plan, and let you report on all the information you've collected, maybe even including overall program evaluation.

Advanced *Case Management* systems can do even more, such as helping with workflow and scheduling. For instance, based on the information you enter about a client, they can recommend that your client meet with a dietician, help to schedule that meeting, and send the dietician a reminder. They can also help to automate your billing processes, particularly if you need to bill government entities or insurance companies.

A number of systems are intended to work across a range of human service scenarios. At the lower-price end of the spectrum, more generic systems such as Apricot and Social Solutions' Efforts to Outcomes (ETO) can provide substantial tracking ability for about $3,000 to $25,000 per year. Somewhat more expensive software, like Tapestry by Visionlink, Bowman Systems' ServicePoint, Service Xpert Suite by Unicentric, or Evolv-CS by Defran, can provide more power for more expense—about $20,000 to $50,000 per year. However, large organizations will likely need to look beyond these tools toward more powerful solutions, like ClientTrack from ClientTrack, Inc.

Those looking to integrate client information with data about their other constituents (like donors), or to support complex and unusual processes, should also consider *Constituent Relationship Management (CRM)* systems. These systems tend to be very flexible, but provide less specialized client-tracking functionality out-of-the-box. For instance, a number of organizations are adapting Salesforce for use in case management, or using Civi-CRM's CiviCase component.

If your programs concentrate on a particular, widely recognized area, such as homeless management, child care, health services, summer camps, or legal aid services, consider tools geared specifically to your type of work. Ask other organizations doing similar work about the tools that they've considered. ●

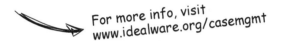

For more info, visit www.idealware.org/casemgmt

Constituent Relationship Management

Constituent Relationship Management (CRM) systems let you manage all of the people your organization interacts with— everyone from donors and volunteers to activists, participants, media contacts, board members, vendors, and more—in a single system. The ideal CRM provides a holistic, person-centric view of all the different ways each person is engaged with your organization, and lets you support all the different ways you reach out to new constituents and grow relationships with them over time.

The right software can make or break a CRM strategy, but what software you choose depends upon your needs. Some tools built specifically as CRMs—like CiviCRM, Salesforce, Microsoft Dynamics CRM, and SugarCRM—support many different types of nonprofit constituents and processes. All of these systems are very flexible, but often need substantial configuration before they can be effectively used. CiviCRM is free and open source, and SugarCRM has a free community version, while Salesforce provides up to 10 free licenses to nonprofits. Microsoft Dynamics CRM offers a substantial nonprofit discount—for larger organizations, it may be cheaper than Salesforce. All four systems typically require IT staff or consultants to get up and running.

If most of your high-priority constituents deal with your organization in a specific way, however, you may be able to implement a CRM strategy more effectively by starting with a system that specializes in that area rather than a more general one. For instance, if fundraising is your highest-priority function and the majority of people you track are donors or potential donors, look for a *Donor Management System* that can also meet most of your other needs. If you do a lot of online outreach and organizing, you might use an *Integrated Online System* as the lynchpin of your CRM strategy. Or, if you're geared primarily around program attendees, build your CRM strategy around a *Membership Management* or a *Case Management* system.

What type of system should you use? If you need to track lots of disparate types of constituents in multiple, complex processes, a generalized CRM system might provide the most flexibility. But if the majority of your needs fall in a particular area—like donor- or client-management—you might start with a system designed for that area, and see if you can expand it to meet your other needs.

Don't discount the possibility of integrating multiple software systems together—for example, working with a developer to use programming interfaces, or APIs—to execute your CRM strategy through two or more connected systems. ●

For more info, visit
www.idealware.org/crm

Thinking Through Your CRM Strategy

In practice, CRM often describes a software strategy and set of processes as much as it does a specific class of software tool. Start by understanding all the different types of constituents you serve, and the types of processes you use to reach and then serve them. What data are you currently storing about constituents (in databases, files, or personal data repositories)? What else would you like to know? What type(s) of systems can help you pull all that data together to get a holistic view of each constituent?

Donor Management

Donor Management software provides specialized function-ality to manage donors, gifts, and prospects. Almost all of these systems let you easily log gifts and track contact information, giving history, and notes. Most also allow you to mail-merge letters, create reports, or query to generate lists of donors. More sophisticated systems offer considerably more functionality for tracking different kinds of gifts—for example, grants, online gifts, major gifts, and planned gifts—and advanced features, but require more technical savvy from fundraisers and IT staff.

Increasingly, many systems include substantial functionality beyond core donor management. Some provide online payment functionality that could potentially replace *Online Donation* or *Event Registration* systems, and others offer some email func-tionality (though it may not be as robust as even inexpensive *Broadcast Email* software). Some donor-management systems move toward the realm of *Constituent Relationship Manage-ment,* providing reasonable functionality to track volunteers, event registrants, or other constituents, in addition to donors.

Inexpensive systems like Blackbaud's eTapestry and Little Green Light start at less than $1,000 per year. Mid-priced systems, like DonorPro, Blackbaud's The Raiser's Edge, and Talisma Fund-raising (formerly Donor2), can cost well over $10,000 to imple-ment. At the high end of the spectrum you could easily spend $100,000 or more.

Regardless of what system you choose, make sure you think through how you will integrate your donor data with other types of constituent data, as many donors likely interact with you in other ways as well. Can you import and export files from the data-base? Are there programming interfaces (called APIs) that allow a programmer to integrate the system with other constituent data systems? Does it make sense to use a very flexible system or a *Constituent Relationship Management* system that can track more than just donors? ●

Buying Additional Data about Your Donors

A number of different vendors can augment the data you've collected about current and potential donors. This service, sometimes called "data appending," starts when you send the vendor basic information, like a name and street address—for a fee, they provide such additional public information as email addresses, more recent addresses, or giving potential.

It's easy to buy nuts-and-bolts information like up-to-date email addresses, physical addresses, phone numbers, or geographic coordinates (for mapping purposes) from services like FreshAddress, TowerData, or Melissa Data. This can be a good way to get information to jumpstart an email- or phone-outreach strategy. Expect the vendor to match just a fraction of your list (perhaps 10-25 percent). Prices vary widely depending on the information you're looking for and the size of your list, but might range from $0.01 to $0.75 per matched name.

You can also buy more detailed demographic data to help assess donors' income levels, often called "wealth screening data." For instance, which donors live in a high-wealth ZIP code, or own yachts? What's the assessed value of their houses (if that information is public)? What political contributions have they made? If you have a very large database, some vendors can even mine your own data to help predict your top prospects.

Wealth screening services like TrueGivers, DonorSearch, DonorTrends, DonorCast, LexisNexis for Development Professionals, WealthPoint, WealthEngine, Blackbaud's Target Analytics, iWave's Prospect Research Online (PRO), and DonorScape offer multiple types of data, and many can provide information on either a single donor (through a web interface) or an entire list.

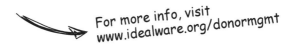

For more info, visit
www.idealware.org/donormgmt

Integrated Online Systems

Integrated Online Systems let nonprofits manage both their web presence and different aspects of constituent information in a single online package. These applications can provide functionality to manage member, donor, and other constituent data, accept online payments, send broadcast emails, manage event registrations, update websites, and more.

Because they're combined into one package, there's no need to sync data between different components, which makes them compelling alternatives to multiple standalone packages. For example, instead of pulling data from both *Broadcast Email* and *Online Donations* tools to sync with your *Donor Management* system, all this information could be stored together in an integrated online system and accessed from a single place.

The downside is that they require more of an investment to buy and set up than individual components. And if you already have a *Donor Management* system in place, you'd need to transfer data to the integrated online system to take advantage of its functionality, a process likely to be fairly complex. These systems are also unlikely to be strong in every area they attempt to cover—look closely at each module to see how it meets your needs.

Prices for integrated tools vary dramatically depending on the number of constituents you track and the features and modules. Several tools, like Wild Apricot, Blackbaud's eTapestry, and Neon by Z2 Systems, start between $25 and $100 per month to support a few hundred constituents, and go up from there. Tools like MemberClicks, Salsa by Salsa Labs, CitySoft, and Artez provide more features for somewhat higher expense. PICnet's Nonprofit Soapbox offers an integrated toolset with consulting help to implement it. Top-of-the-market software like Blackbaud's Sphere and Luminate provides rich toolsets for sizable national nonprofits. ●

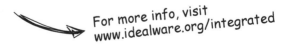

For more info, visit
www.idealware.org/integrated

Volunteer Management Software

Do you work with a lot of volunteers, and track their hours, interests, schedules, and contributions? If so, you'll want a system that can help with those tasks and maybe even help you recruit people and collect information about potential volunteers online.

It's important to think carefully, though, as to whether a system specifically devoted only to managing volunteers makes sense for you. Volunteers are frequently also donors, event attendees, or even clients as well, so tracking them in their own standalone system can create unnecessary data headaches.

Instead, it probably makes sense to look to *Constituent Relationship Management (CRM)* software, a *Donor Management* system, or an *Integrated Online System* that can also track volunteer data. *CRMs* like Salesforce and CiviCRM are typically, by definition, flexible enough to track and report on many different kinds of data, including volunteer information. Alternatively, a number of *Donor Management* or *Integrated Online Systems* have modules with solid support for volunteer tracking— for example, GiftWorks, DonorPro, Sage's Fundraising 50 and Fundraising 100, and Blackbaud's The Raiser's Edge and Sphere. Some *Association Management* systems may also be flexible enough to track volunteer information.

If you have very complicated scheduling needs, or complex recruiting processes, it's possible that a specific *Volunteer Management* tool like the Volunteer Reporter, Samaritan eRecruiter/eCoordinator, or Volgistics will be helpful. These systems can track volunteer certifications, background checks, hours worked, and even assign time slots based on skills and availability (for example, who has a third-class driver's license and is available Thursday afternoons?). Make sure you know how you'll manage your data to consider your volunteers as potential donors or event participants. Otherwise, you've lost the ability to see all their interactions with your organization. ●

Recruiting Volunteers Online

Want to put the word out that you're looking for volunteers? Online sites like VolunteerMatch.org and Idealist.org allow you to post opportunities to large communities of potential volunteers—they're essentially job boards for volunteers.

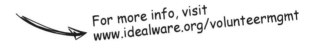
For more info, visit
www.idealware.org/volunteermgmt

Specialized Constituent Management Systems

From churches to homeless shelters, there are organizations that have specialized constituent tracking needs. Some organizations choose to implement software targeted at their specific type of nonprofit, while others customize *Donor Management, Membership Management,* or *Constituent Relationship Management* systems to suit their needs. We profile some specialized types in this section, but there are more-- it's worth investigating what constituent tracking software is targeted at your specific sector.

Attendance Tracking Systems

For nonprofits with a high number of walk-in clients—such as community centers, drop-ins, or libraries and museums—simply counting who comes in the door is important, and almost always too complex to record by manual processes. Organizations that don't sell tickets might derive this data from *Attendance Tracking Systems.*

No matter what the underlying technology of the system might be, *Attendance Tracking Systems* work on the principle of unique identifiers, either a numeric code in the case of systems that simply count who walks in the door, or a physical, scannable object. If a scannable device or other check-in process is involved, the time of each scan is captured and linked to a member's database record (or a client's or patron's). However, that "swipe" data also lives apart from the database record as a unique piece of information, and can be analyzed—how many people came in at 6 a.m. in February versus 6 a.m. in August, for instance?

While inconceivable to most nonprofits, more-advanced gate counting technologies exist. Radio Frequency Identification (RFID) allows you to track visitors without actively scanning anything—a sensor in the room counts each person as they enter using a small chip in their ID card. Another potential high-tech method is biometric scanning—for example, scanning a constituent's fingerprint to grant them access to a room—but most nonprofits aren't anywhere near this level of technological sophistication. Typically, the scanner or other counting equipment you use will be connected to a computer to automatically record each visitor. If you need to scan attendees away from a computer—for example, at an outdoor event—most scanners should be able to instead store the data on a USB flash drive. Organizations that can't afford special equipment, or that don't rely on attendance tracking for most of their programs but need to capture this information more occasionally, might simply record the data in a *Spreadsheet* or explore *Mobile Apps* to help with head counts. Depending on your program needs, you might find an *Attendance Tracking System* packaged as just one part of a larger set of software, like CCC's OpTIME for YMCAs and similar organizations.

Church Management Systems

The church management software sector is sophisticated and thriving, and vendors in the sector have begun to incorporate innovations from other systems marketed to handle general nonprofit data management. Vendors here often specialize in the mainline Protestant, Catholic, and evangelical denominations and the particular data needs of each. Some larger companies, like Shelby and ACS Technology, market different products to each of these sectors. The landscape is varied, with both installed and cloud-based options. Most churches gauge size depending on average weekend attendance, and will choose a solution based on that benchmark. Megachurches, defined as those that have more than 2,000 people come to worship on average each weekend, have their own special data management needs, and are also accommodated by the marketplace.

Church Management systems generally focus on helping staff keep track of the individuals and households who come to worship services and events; broadcast email and direct mail management; fundraising efforts; Sunday schools and prayer groups; and reporting on finances, programs, and attendance. Some of the systems on the market, like Church Windows and Shelby, help manage HR and payroll, too. The sector is robust enough to merit its own publication, Christian Computing Magazine, which publishes a helpful online chart comparing the products and their features every October.

Like other nonprofits, churches are increasingly interested in building relationships with their constituents, and many systems are moving toward a *Constituent Relationship Management* strategy. Staffers at churches tend to be drawn to the mission of the organization and aren't always the most tech-savvy, so a user-friendly system is a must. Many *Church Management* systems have robust support packages in recognition of this. For some churches, it's important for the software to be available on a mobile platform and integrated seamlessly into their website.

Custom Databases

Despite the plethora of software systems available for nonprofits to handle specialized needs, some organizations have chosen to build databases from scratch (or close to scratch) to track their constituent information. Although *Custom Databases* like these aren't always the most nimble, many organizations continue to maintain them rather than deal with converting to new solutions.

Although these systems are powerful, they can be clunky when an organization is attempting to tailor them to new workflows— for instance, if a new grant comes in. There's often not a ton of expertise on staff to alter the framework of the database. As a result, these systems should be considered a last-resort solution when your organization can't find a specialized database, or your data is too complex or unusual to track in an off-the-shelf system. However, *Custom Databases* might make sense if you're tracking a lot of "flat," non-relational information and have too much to keep in a spreadsheet. If you're looking to track information about people involved with your programs, though—constituents or clients with multiple points of interaction with your organization—*Custom Databases* might not be the right system, as you won't be able to track very sophisticated relationships.

For smaller datasets, two of the most commonly-used *Custom Databases* are Microsoft Access, which is available on its own or as part of Microsoft Office, and Filemaker Pro. Both are relatively inexpensive but will require significant time to customize to your needs. For more robust tracking of larger datasets—those with around 10,000 entries or more—you can also look to more powerful enterprise-level solutions, like Oracle or Microsoft SQL.

Electronic Medical Records

Substantial privacy and confidentiality issues surround patient data stored in *Electronic Medical Records (EMR)* systems. As such, most EMR systems aren't appropriate for most multi-service organizations' all-in-one database solutions. Although some of this data will be similar to information tracked in *Case Management* databases, much of it—like test results and prescription information—should not be tracked with other data in shared systems because of confidentiality concerns.

As part of the Affordable Care Act, health care providers are being mandated to convert from paper to electronic medical and health records software by 2015 or pay a penalty. Additionally, providers who bill Medicare or Medicaid receive a financial incentive to convert before the deadline. This legal change has led to an influx of new EMR software systems in the marketplace. Many are being marketed to nonprofit organizations with limited budgets that will need to extract information about programs from their EMR systems to report to the government or private funders. Few of these integrate seamlessly with widely used *Case Management* systems, and few agencies have the budget to set up a system integration or deploy a *Middleware* solution. This can lead to the problem of manual double-entry, and can make tracking data relating to programs more complex. Some multi-service organizations use a *CRM* system like Salesforce to track medical information, which makes integration with a *Case Management* system more feasible.

Legal Case Management Systems

Legal aid organizations need software to help track their clients, manage billable hours, handle pro bono referrals, and lots more. In many instances, this means *Legal Case Management Systems* developed specifically for the legal sector—in this context, "case" refers to a court case rather than groups of constituents. Some legal nonprofits also use their *Legal Case Management Systems* to track foundation proposals and prospects, but for the most part, that's handled by an external system that's fairly siloed. Unique to *Legal Case Management Systems* is the document assembly capabilities that many of them offer, which allow paralegals and attorneys to work with clients to create complex legal documents by prompts and fill-ins offered by the software. At the end of the interview process, clients have a legal document they can take with them to court appointments or for future filings. Legal aid organizations often use *Legal Case Management Systems* to manage electronic case files, and sometimes built-in questionnaires have the capability to help automate the intake process with branching criteria. Some systems offer conflict of interest checking, too.

There are only a handful of *Legal Case Management Systems* on the market, with big names including Kemp's Case Works, Legal Files, and Pika Software. If you're a legal aid organization, you probably already have a *Legal Case Management System*, but it's worth checking out its reporting capabilities and interoperability with other systems.

Library and Collection Management Systems

Libraries, museums, and archives need to keep track of more than just people, including the books, artifacts, and other pieces of cultural heritage that make up the organizations' holdings. These institutions might use an Integrated Library System (ILS), *Library Management System,* or Collection Management System to evaluate programs such as backlog processing, grant-based preservation and conservation work, provenance research, removing old or underused items from collections, and more.

Many larger academic and public libraries use different ILS modules to manage patron, acquisitions, and circulation data. The system can also be used for cataloging items and serials—both digital and physical—into collections as well as to maintain the public catalog interface that patrons navigate, either from within the library or remotely. Sometimes the ILS can also manage the digital assets in an institution's holdings, like scanned documents or oral history recordings. Bigger institutions often use proprietary software like Aleph or Voyager from Ex Libris (Voyager was formerly a product of Endeavor), or Millenium from Innovative Interfaces.

Some institutions, including smaller libraries that previously lacked the resources to implement a proprietary ILS, are exploring newer open source offerings like VuFind, created by Villanova University, or Evergreen, originally developed by the Georgia State Library. These systems require significant staff time to get up and running, but once your collection data is in them, an institution won't be charged money to use the systems and can use the system to serve as a central repository for all collections and patron data.

Special collections libraries and archives, which usually don't have materials that circulate and require substantial original cataloging and description data, might be included in the ILS but often also have dedicated systems (most often homegrown) with substantial additional data. The two most widely-used open source systems,

Archon and Archivist's Toolkit, are working toward merging as ArchivesSpace, an open source archival Content Management System.

Museums and historical societies also need systems to capture data about their collections and patrons. PastPerfect has traditionally been the most popular catalog and accession system for small historical societies. The more expensive Argus, The Museum System (TMS), and KE Emu have been widely adopted by larger institutions.

Student Information Systems

Nonprofits that operate full-fledged academic institutions, like charter schools, use a dedicated database called a SIS, or *Student Information System*. A SIS tracks notably different information than a *Learning Management System (LMS)*, which helps manage curriculum. A SIS holds data including students' completed credits and their progress toward degrees. Usually, they are packaged with online portals that can help a student or their parents monitor this information themselves. They also often have modules that track tuition and financial aid, facility management, alumni information, and prospecting and admissions. For institutions that teach younger kids, keeping track of attendance and disciplinary actions is more important. K-12 schools might use SunGard's eSchoolPLUS or Pearson's PowerSchool, while higher education institutions could choose from Oracle's PeopleSoft Campus Solutions or Ellucian's Banner.

Synagogue Management Systems

Some synagogues choose to implement software specifically designed for their needs. The majority of synagogues function on a membership basis, so it's critical that the staff has a system that can help them keep track of which households have paid their dues and which haven't.

Like other nonprofit organizations, fundraising is critical to a synagogue's mission. *Synagogue Management* software can help synagogue staffers manage gifts, pledges, tributes, and honorary donations. Specific to Judaism is the concept of Yahrzeits, in which congregants come to services in order to honor the anniversary of a loved one's death. Friends and relatives will often make a donation in honor of a Yahrzeit, and the system can help the process by generating a letter notifying them of the upcoming anniversary and suggesting a donation. These anniversaries can be commemorated using either the Gregorian or the Hebrew calendar, so synagogue management systems should ideally accommodate both.

Synagogues have complex accounting needs, and synagogue management systems should export seamlessly to a general ledger tool. Many tools now offer broadcast email integration so that staffers can keep their congregation in the loop, too.

The high holidays are traditionally the busiest time for synagogues, and other events like speaker series or special dinners are a key part of these organizations' programming. Members increasingly want to register and pay for these events online. Some systems on the market allow synagogues to integrate the tools into their websites, and accept payment directly through them. A few synagogue management systems have fancy box office-style seat selection, while most have more basic functionality like overflow tracking.

Many synagogues have Hebrew school (for older children) and religious school (for younger children), and *Synagogue Management* software can help keep track of data like grades, attendance, and emergency contact information if a more substantial student management system isn't quite appropriate. Some synagogues manage cemeteries, too, and will need their database to manage plots, reservations, and billings for those properties.

The *Synagogue Management* software universe is witnessing something of a transition. There are more established vendors in this space, who have been around for decades and usually offer systems built upon installed systems with optional web-based components, like MM2000 and Chaverware. There are also newer solutions that have harnessed the power of *Constituent Relationship Management (CRM)* platforms and built specific products on top of them, like ShulSuite and Cloud for Synagogues. As relationship building becomes more important to congregations, systems are beginning to adapt their underpinnings to fit this model, and are offering a more customizable, networked solution to synagogues. ●

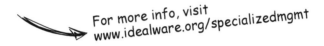
For more info, visit
www.idealware.org/specializedmgmt

It's a fact of life: as a nonprofit, you need to raise money. Whether you're raising it from individual donors or grants or through galas or conferences, software can help you raise money and lower your stress level at the same time.

All of the software names highlighted within the text are covered in more detail in this guide. Most of them are included in this section, and follow immediately after the descriptions.

If you're interested in a software type and can't find it in this section, you can look it up in the Index.

Whether your primary funding sources are individual donors or grants, fundraising is important to almost every nonprofit—and there's a lot of software that can help.

Strongly consider...

Enlisting major donors, foundations, or corporate sponsors often involves a substantial cultivation process. An advanced *Donor Management* or *Constituent Relationship Management* system can provide such useful features as the ability to track specific foundation interests, create contact logs, generate call reminders, and help guide staff through specific cultivation processes. While you can use separate systems to manage donors, online donations, and broadcast email, you'll need to synchronize and integrate data between them. Some organizations may find it useful to instead use a single *Integrated Online System* that manages all this information in one place. These systems are covered in our Constituent Management section.

Most fundraising programs can benefit from an online component. To get started, you'll need *Online Donation* software that lets you accept credit cards online, either for one-time donations or on a recurring basis. *Broadcast Email* tools facilitate the email outreach that can inspire prospective donors to give (more on those in our One-Way Communications section). You can also find opportunities to connect your organization with philanthropies online through *Foundation Grant Research.*

If you want to take users' credit card information for member-ships, donations, purchases, or other transactions, you'll find a number of affordable *Credit Card Processing Systems* (covered in Back Office and Productivity) that can make such tasks pain-less and secure.

Keeping ahead of the curve...

Enlisting staff, volunteers, or close friends to help fundraise is common practice. Several tools are available to help manage the logistics involved. *Peer-to-Peer Fundraising* lets supporters create their own online-fundraising web pages, and can support your organization in managing this kind of distributed campaign.

Social networking sites like *Facebook* and *Twitter,* as well as LinkedIn and Google+, can also provide some aid in raising money through networks, though organizations generally find them more effective as outreach tools. *Photo and Video Sharing* tools can also help you spread interest about your organization's mission and get your supporters fired up. Learn more about these tools in our Two-Way Communications section.

On the cutting edge...

Crowdfunding is a strategy that's gaining traction with some nonprofits. Sites that support the funding of a project until a goal has been met have emerged as a real force, especially in the cultural and arts sectors. Large organizations have also begun to experiment with fundraising by *Mobile Text Messaging* campaigns, which let donors give small amounts by sending a specific text message from mobile phones—a strategy discussed further in our One-Way Communications section. ●

From fundraising galas and get-to-know-you gatherings to educational workshops and conferences, events are often an integral part of fundraising and marketing plans. The right software can help you promote and manage them.

Strongly consider...

In the weeks leading up to an event, you'll want to promote it, both on your website and through the outreach methods described in the Reaching Out to New Friends and Engaging Current Supporters sections. In addition, think through the various events calendars on which you could post the event—many existing online communities include calendars, and a *Web Content Management System* (in our One-way Communications section) can help you create one on your own site and even manage registrations. Social networking sites like *Facebook* or *Twitter* (in the Two-Way Communications section) can also help you post your calendar of events.

Event Registration software can be helpful both to track information about who's planning to attend an event, and to allow online payments for events with a registration fee. More sophisticated systems can also help manage details like meal preferences, name tags, workshop sign-ups, different pricing levels, or even on-site registration. Some *Donor Management Systems* and *Integrated Online Systems* can help manage registrations, too, but they're typically not as sophisticated in this functionality as dedicated systems—learn more in our Constituent Management section.

Many events also require some kind of printed pieces, including programs, schedules, or organizational information. *Page Layout* tools, profiled in our Back Office and Productivity section, can help you create professional and polished materials that best represent your organization.

Keeping ahead of the curve...

Managing the logistics of a complex event can be daunting. Dedicated *Event and Auction Management* software can provide sophisticated support for tracking schedules, budgets, auctions, sponsors, and all the other details that go into planning. *Online Auctions* can add an interesting online component to your event, as well.

If you're an arts organization and you host performances with assigned seats—like theater events, for example—you may want a *Ticketing* system, especially one that integrates with your donor or constituent database.

On the cutting edge...

At a large, live event, it can be interesting to let attendees post questions live and then project and view them online via *Online Chat* tools (covered in Collaboration) or using *Twitter* (in Two-Way Communications). These same tools can also be useful to facilitate live discussion with distributed audiences. ●

Crowdfunding

Crowdfunding, or Crowd-Sourced Fundraising, tools often contain many of the same features as standard *Peer-to-Peer Fundraising* tools, with one important difference—in addition to allowing nonprofits to reach out to current supporters and invite them to fundraise on the organization's behalf, crowd-sourced tools offer access to a homegrown network of people interested in supporting compelling projects.

Individuals join the "crowd" using a specific tool, search the charities and other projects posted there, and make donations—frequently to organizations with which they have no established relationship. Often these tools cater to a specific mission area, like arts, education, or progressive causes, and most rely on innovative funding models to encourage their community of donors to participate and rally around a cause.

There are two major players in this software market for nonprofits to consider. Kickstarter is a crowd-sourcing tool used to find funding for arts, music, films, and other creative projects. Users post projects along with their goals and a timeframe, and the community pledges money. Keep in mind that the site can only be used to fund a project, and not to raise money for general operating. Typically the projects will offer something in the way of rewards or thank-you gifts to donors, depending on how much is pledged, and they link quickly to *Facebook* and *Twitter*. It's important to note that Kickstarter works on an all-or-nothing basis. If your project doesn't meet its goal by the deadline, you don't get any money, and all of your donors are refunded in full, a policy designed to motivate nonprofits to fundraise and supporters to donate. While free to use, Kickstarter takes 5 percent of what you raise in fees, in addition to the credit card processing fees from Amazon Payments, if your project is successful.

Indiegogo is similar to Kickstarter, but it lets you choose between an all-or-nothing funding model or one in which you keep all the money you raise, even if you don't meet your fundraising goal. If you meet your fundraising goal, the fee charged by Indiegogo ends up at 4 percent of the total amount raised; if you don't meet your goal but still wish to keep the money you raised, Indiegogo charges a 9 percent fee. A credit card processing fee of 3 percent also applies. Registered 501(c)3 nonprofits, however, get a 25 percent discount. ●

For more info, visit www.idealware.org/crowdfunding

Come on Over to My House

House parties and meet ups are opportunities for committed supporters to host parties or similar events to raise money for you or your cause. With the right software, organizers can publicize their parties, while others who share their cause can search a central list of events being hosted in order to find those of interest. Participants can also RSVP, allowing organizers to get a count of who's coming. You can use an Integrated **Online System,** your **Web Content Management System,** an **Event Registration** system, or a standalone **Peer-to-Peer Fundraising** system to manage these events.

Event and Auction Management

Planning events and auctions involves a lot of logistics, including sponsors, budgets, schedules, seating, and facilities. Some *Donor Management* systems, *Constituent Relationship Management* systems, *Membership Management* software, and even some *Volunteer Management* systems can help with these tasks. It's useful to have this functionality integrated with other constituent management functions, but the features these tools provide is rarely as sophisticated as in dedicated packages.

Good *Event Registration* software often not only helps your attendees register online, but has event-management capabilities as well—for instance, to assign seats or manage schedules and rooms. Very high-end tools like StarCite and etouches provide both event registration and sophisticated management capabilities with functionality designed to help you to track complex logistics, speakers, rooms, and budgets for huge events and conferences. It's very convenient to have management functionality combined with your online registration tool.

Live and silent auctions often require tracking particularly complex sets of information, including the items for sale, their fair market value, buyers, and selling prices, plus the need to generate bills and receipts on-site within minutes of each sale. Dedicated *Auction Management* packages like Greater Giving's Auctionpay and ReadySetAuction provide functionality tailored specifically to these needs. ●

 For more info, visit idealware.org/eventmgmt

Event Management, or Event Planner?

Keep in mind that no software will actually plan all the details for you—if your logistics become more complicated than what you can easily manage by yourself using mid-priced **Event Registration** software or an Excel spreadsheet, you might consider hiring an experienced event planner.

Event Registration

These days, people expect to be able to register for events online. With the right software, you can accept RSVPs, manage attendee information, and accept payment, all online.

For simple RSVP-only needs that don't require the exchange of money, free tools like Evite, Eventbrite, and Paperless Post, or even SurveyMonkey or Google Drive forms, provide the ability to understand who's coming, with a little flexibility in how your registration form looks and what information it collects. The *Facebook* Events application is another interesting option if most of your constituents use the social networking site. Or, you could set up a form on your own website—a straightforward process using a module available with your *Web Content Management System.*

If you need to collect registration fees, PayPal, Eventbrite, or Brown Paper Tickets can provide basic functionality with minimal fees. A number of packages, including Click & Pledge, Greater Giving, Formstack, Qgiv, GiftTool, and MemberClicks, support a variety of other transaction types in addition to events like donations and online-store sales. These tools all charge fees that generally come to about 2.5 percent to 4 percent of the transaction, and some also have recurring fees ranging from $20 to $500 per month.

More sophisticated tools like 123Signup, RegOnline, and Cvent add support for such additional features as customizing registration page look-and-feel, multi-track conference registration, complex discounts, name-tag generation, sophisticated reporting, and more. Typical pricing includes transaction fees between 2.5 percent and 4 percent of the fee plus $1-4 per registration.

A number of *Donor Management, Constituent Relationship Management, Web Content Management Systems,* and *Integrated Online Systems* support *Event Registration.* This is also a common function in *Membership Management Systems.* ●

For more resources, see www.idealware.org/eventreg

EVENT REGISTRATION

Foundation Grant Research

At its most basic, grant prospect research essentially consists of two major practices: researching various foundations' grant cycles and giving histories, and managing your organization's applications for each foundation. The former is essentially an exercise in web research—identifying a list of foundations that might give to your organization and locating them online to identify the types of organizations they've funded in the past, and with what size grants—and the latter is a matter of tracking and managing data.

When looking up giving histories and grant cycles, websites like the Foundation Center Database or GrantStation allow you to search very detailed records of foundations by a variety of criteria, including past grants, focus areas, and giving interests. You can also look to your state nonprofit association, as many will offer access to these tools at a substantial discount. Alternatively, many regional or local philanthropy centers offer access as a benefit of membership, or free on-location in their "grant-research libraries."

In addition, regional associations of grantmakers can be valuable sources. Most grantmaker associations, also known as philanthropy centers, will house a publicly available list of foundations specific to a geographic area. Some are print-only, but a number offer online databases as well. You can also find associations of grantmakers centered around a mission area, such as Grantmakers in Film and Electronic Media, or on other criteria, like the Association of Small Foundations. Searching member lists for these associations may help identify potential grant prospects.

Federal grants are another key source of funding for many organizations. While you won't find these grants in private and corporate foundation databases, you can search for United States federal grant opportunities at grants.gov. State and local grant listings can most often be found on your municipality's website. A basic web search is also a great way to find out what grants nonprofits similar to your own have received that yours may qualify for. Many nonprofits list foundation funders on their websites or in annual reports.

Once you've identified a list of foundations, you'll need to determine their giving histories and grant capacities. While the Foundation Center dataset will have a lot of this information, you may also need to search in other places to find everything you're looking for. Sites like GuideStar let you search a database that contains more than five million IRS Forms 990—the form the government uses to track financial information about organizations. You'll have to know how to read a 990, however. A number of helpful sites can show you how, including the Nonprofit Coordinating Committee of New York's web page.

As you collect this information, you'll need a place to store it. Smaller organizations can usually accomplish this through a spreadsheet, like in Microsoft Excel or Google Drive, just creating columns to track foundation information, web links, interests, and due dates for RFPs and proposals. Most *Donor Management Systems* will also let you manage your list of foundations just like any other prospect, as well as track RFP and proposal dates, the status of your proposals, and your proposal workflows. If you have very detailed needs around managing grant application processes and requirements, consider a standalone system like Abila Grant Management, Philantech's Philantrack, or IT Works.

In addition, it can be useful to supplement your deadline- and submission-date records with *Email and Calendar Software* or task-management software that can function as a to-do list to ensure you don't miss any deadlines or get caught by surprise. ●

For more resources,
see www.idealware.org/grantresearch

Online Auctions

Holding an *Online Auction* can be an interesting fundraising technique for a nonprofit, particularly as an adjunct to a live event. They work similarly to traditional auctions—potential bidders browse web pages to see pictures, descriptions, and suggested prices for auction items, and bid by entering the amount they're willing to pay. When the auction ends, the highest bidder wins the item.

MissionFish works with the popular online auction site eBay to allow nonprofits to conduct auctions for little to no charge. Listings are available to anyone who searches eBay, which lets you take advantage of the huge audience, but makes it difficult to create a special event feel or to build community.

Other tools, such as ReadySetAuction, CharityBuzz, and Bidding-ForGood, are specifically designed for a more "special event" auction feel. They're more expensive than MissionFish, but offer more customized auction homepages and the ability to add sponsor logos. With these tools, you'll need to drive your own constituents to purchase the items (as opposed to relying on an existing audience, like eBay's), but they are designed to help you create a community feel around your auction. ●

 For more info, visit www.idealware.org/auctions

Want to Combine On- and Offline Auctions?

Conducting an event that involves both on- and offline auctions can expand your audience. ReadySetAuction and Greater Giving (with online auction functionality powered by BiddingForGood) both provide functionality to integrate the two.

Online Donations

Online Donation software allows you to easily accept credit card payments over the web. Almost all of these tools work the same way—a "donate" button on your website links to a donation form where donors enter contact and credit card information. The tool verifies and charges the credit card securely, and makes sure the money reaches your organization. Online reporting tools let you see what's been donated and export the donation information to other databases.

Many standalone tools can take *Online Donations*—in fact, many can also help with a number of different types of online payments, like membership or registration fees. If you're just starting out, some tools—like Click & Pledge or Network for Good's DonateNow Lite—charge no monthly fees, just a percentage of the donations you receive. Other tools like PayPal and Amazon Payments are even cheaper, but are tailored more for item sales than for donations. You can also use an online form tool like Wufoo, if you're up for the configuration process.

If you expect to receive more than a few donations, it might make more sense to pay a monthly rate in exchange for a lower percentage fee, like $20-$40 a month for 3-3.5 percent. Tools like Click & Pledge, Greater Giving, GiftTool, Network for Good's DonateNow, or Qgiv are also more feature-rich, offering more support for different types of gifts, customized donation forms, and faster donation receipt.

If you're interested in tools that enable supporters to accept donations for you on their own sites, consider *Peer-to-Peer Fundraising* tools. Dwolla, an online payment network, will let you take payments via your Facebook page or Twitter posts.

If you use a standalone tool, you'll need to export donor information into whatever system you're using to manage donors, which can be a substantial process if you receive a lot of donations. Instead, many organizations use *Donor Management, Constituent Relationship Management,* or *Integrated Online Systems* that support both online donations and the management of donor data. ●

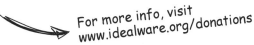 For more info, visit www.idealware.org/donations

Peer-to-Peer Fundraising

Peer-to-Peer Fundraising, also called online distributed fund-raising, group fundraising, team fundraising, or widget fundraising, involves recruiting supporters—including staff members, core volunteers, or passionate advocates—to fundraise for an organization. This technique can result in a lot of new donors, but since they're often personally connected to the individual fundraiser rather than the organization, they may not be as likely to participate in other programs or to give multiple times.

Many *Peer-to-Peer Fundraising* tools—including FirstGiving, Razoo, CrowdRise, and StayClassy—let potential fundraisers create their own personalized fundraising pages, and all offer a version that's free except for a percentage of donations. Pages can have customized pictures, text, and easy links to give money online, and can stand alone or be associated with particular events, like walk-a-thons. Individual fundraisers direct their own friends and family to their pages and take donations. The Causes app (from Causes.com) makes it easy to add a fundraising element to your *Facebook* page, although recent changes within that social media platform mean that you may see less success there than even a few years ago.

More sophisticated tools also let organizational staff members easily oversee a campaign's progress or organize fundraisers into teams. Blackbaud's Friends Asking Friends and TeamRaiser (formerly Convio) or the tools offered by Artez Interactive, for instance, provide more sophisticated—though considerably more expensive—organizational support in a standalone package. A number of *Integrated Online Systems* and *Donor Management* tools also offer some of this functionality.

Peer-to-Peer Fundraising takes more than just the right tool, however. It takes planning, experience, and staff time to create and run a successful fundraising campaign. A good peer-to-peer campaign starts with a strong community of supporters motivated and excited about helping your organization raise money. It's not enough to just pick a tool and turn your supporters loose with it—you'll need to train them to use the tool and to be effective fundraisers, and support them throughout the process with helpful tips, success stories, or inspirational quotes. And once your campaign has ended, you need to recognize them for all the work they've put in to make it a success. ●

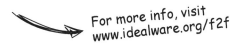

For more info, visit
www.idealware.org/f2f

What About Crowdsourcing?

If your organization has an active online community, you may want to consider crowdfunding, or crowdsourced fundraising. To learn about Crowdsourcing, see page 171.

Ticketing

Ticketing is a complicated area, with the potential of a lot of advanced requirements. You don't need to be a very large arts venue to want to be able to sell tickets to reserved seats. And pretty much any organization would want to consider patrons who have bought tickets as donors. But when you put these two together, it makes for a complex and often expensive system.

At the lowest end of the spectrum, you can use the same vendors as you would use for paid event registration. Vendors in this space, like TicketLeap, Eventbrite, or Brown Paper Tickets allow you to sell tickets online, including different levels of tickets to the same event (like VIP or mezzanine tickets). (For a broader overview, see *Event Registration.*)

If you just need to sell reserved seats for your venue, and it's not critical to you to easily pull your event patrons into your fundraising process, there's a lot of small online software that will allow you to sell tickets. These websites—like OvationTix, Tix, TixHub, Ticket Turtle, and Vendini—allow you to sell tickets, often including box office functionality to print tickets to box office printers. New Concept Software's Tick-It! Trak Pro and Center Stage Software's WinTix/WebTix provide both installed box office software and online solutions.

Even for a small organization, it can be very useful to have a single system that allows you to track not just tickets but also the full fundraising process. Easy-Ware's Total Info and Arts Management Systems' Theatre Manager provide affordable installed software with integrated online ticketing functionality.

In addition, it can be valuable for organizations of all sizes to track their patrons with their other constituents in a *CRM.* For small to medium sized organizations, PatronManager is built on top of the Salesforce platform and includes reserved seating ticketing and box-office functionality. Choice Ticketing Systems and AudienceView Ticketing provide more sophisticated functionality and provide some constituent tracking functionality for medium sized and larger organizations. Paciolan also provides ticketing and fundraising functionality for larger organizations, and Blackbaud's The Patron Edge also provides box office functionality, with some ability to integrate into The Raiser's Edge.

For the arts management world, Tessitura provides functionality that integrates complex box office, online ticketing, and fundraising. It's a complex system that's more appropriate for organizations with multimillion dollar budgets than for small ones, and requires considerable customization, training, and staff time to use.

If you have complex box office needs but don't need a lot of fundraising functionality, you may find that the ticketing systems used primarily by stadiums and commercial venues work well for your needs. These systems, like ProVenue by Tickets.com, Ticketmaster Classic, or Ticketmaster Archtics, tend to not offer much sophisticated functionality to track donor interactions, pledges, or a donation made with an event payment, but instead focus on complex online and offline box office functionality needed by venue. ●

For more info, visit www.idealware.org/ticketing

To build your base, you'll need to reach out to find new supporters. There are a number of ways to get your story out there to make it easier for people find you. From software to help with Podcasts and Infographics to such cutting-edge communications methods as Mobile Apps or online Geolocation platforms, there are tools to help any nonprofit.

All of the software names highlighted within the text are covered in more detail in this guide. Most of them are included in this section, and follow immediately after the descriptions. If you're interested in a software type and can't find it in this section, you can look it up in the Index.

Successful outreach to find new supporters, donors, volunteers, clients, or other friends begins with an effective, compelling story. Start with the *Web Content Management System* and *Broadcast Email* tools covered in the Every Organization Needs section to communicate what makes your organization interesting.

Strongly consider...

Printed postcards or brochures can effectively spread the word about your organization. *Page Layout* tools help you create these materials with a professional, polished design—read more about those in our Back Office and Productivity section.

Your website can also be a strong ally in recruiting new supporters. Investing in a *Mobile Website* will help make sure that visitors on their phones and tablets have the best possible experience. Make sure people interested in your cause can find your site through Google or other search engines by using *Search Engine Optimization (SEO)* techniques.

A solid *Constituent Relationship Management* system is invaluable in tracking new constituents—whether as names on a direct mailing list, those that have signed up online, or people you've had direct contact with. A good software package will help you segment out the people you'd like to contact and track which outreach methods are working. Learn more in our Constituent Management section.

Social networking sites like *Facebook* and *Twitter* can also provide interesting ways to reach out beyond your own network to your friends' friends online. *LinkedIn* can not only help you meet new people—including volunteers, board members, constituents, and other like-minded people—but offers some interesting possibilities for discussions. These tools are discussed in our Two-Way Communications section.

Charts, Diagrams, and *Infographics* provide a visually appealing means of conveying data to your audience. And any organization that needs its constituents to take action should consider *eAdvocacy* tools, too—consider creating *Petitions* or *Pledges* and asking your supporters to sign on.

Keeping ahead of the curve...

Getting people talking about your resources, cause, or message is great—and better yet if they pass it on to their own networks. While there's no guaranteed method to create a viral success, you can increase your chances by making sure your message is compelling and accessible online.

Your executive director, staff, or subject matter experts might keep regularly updated *Blogs*—but remember that this particular technology takes a lot of care and feeding. You can also post your resources to *Video* or *Photo Sharing Websites.* All of these technologies are discussed in the Two-Way Communications section. *Podcasts,* regularly published audio or video programs, can also be ways to reach select audiences.

Don't forget about advertising. *Online Advertising* possibilities offer affordable means for even small organizations to reach large audiences.

On the cutting edge...

Geolocation sites like FourSquare and social media sites that have built-in geolocation capabilities, like Facebook and Twitter, can give your physical location an online presence. They also have the power to engage visitors and attendees—we'll talk more about this strategy in Two-Way Communications.

Though not as buzzed-about as they were a few years ago, some nonprofits are using *QR Codes,* or square bar codes that can be scanned using smart phone cameras, in interesting ways, including direct mail and newsletters.

Some larger organizations have found success building *Mobile Apps*—although we don't recommend that smaller nonprofits take on such an expensive and complicated enterprise. A mobile strategy more in reach for all nonprofits is *Mobile Text Messaging,* which might be a smart way to stay in touch, especially if your constituents prefer communicating by SMS. ●

Broadcast Email

Broadcast Email software lets you email a group of people all at once—as many as you want. It also helps you create attractive emails (often through graphic templates), manage email address lists, and let people subscribe and unsubscribe by themselves. In addition, more advanced tools help you collect email addresses on your website, "mail-merge" information into emails, send messages to particular segments of your mailing list grouped by demographics, and report on how many recipients opened or clicked on each email.

VerticalResponse is a good option in this area, offering nonprofits a sophisticated feature-set and up to 10,000 emails for free. Mail-Chimp also has a product donation program for nonprofits. Other options include Constant Contact, Campaign Monitor, and iContact. WhatCounts provides compelling premium services targeted at those sending hundreds of thousands of emails a month.

Note that many *Donor Management, Constituent Relationship Management,* and *Integrated Online Systems* provide some Broadcast Email functionality. While not all can match the advanced features of dedicated software, you may find that your existing software meets your needs. It's also worth setting up an integration between your constituent management solution and your Broadcast Email provider to get a more holistic picture of your supporters. ●

For more info, visit
www.idealware.org/email

Take Care with Installed Packages

If you email more than a few dozen people at a time, use an offsite vendor that supports mass emails. Tools like Outlook aren't designed to support large-scale mailings, and won't help with the formatting and list-management tasks critical for large lists. When you use them to email hundreds of people, you may reach more Spam filters than inboxes—or worse, your mail server might be blacklisted as Spam, blocking future emails from anyone in your organization.

Charts, Diagrams, and Infographics

There's a reason people say pictures are worth a thousand words. Graphical depictions of data or processes can convey the main message and a host of supporting information in a single glance—in a way most audiences will find unintimidating, interesting, and easy to follow. With a building interest in infographics, it's even possible that your visualizations will be passed around and reach a substantial new audience.

It's often useful to create charts to represent data in an understandable way. Google Drive Spreadsheet and Many Eyes provide tools geared toward creating interactive online charts inexpensively, or even for free. These online tools, however, offer considerably less power to create charts that are substantial enough for printed publications. Microsoft Excel, SmartDraw, and DeltaGraph provide powerful functionality to create printed charts, and they're all under $200 for nonprofits. Tableau offers sophisticated online and offline software geared toward those with more complex needs and a higher budget. For more complicated visualizations, you'll either need *Statistical Analysis Tools* for more mathematic power, or the advanced graphic abilities of design software like Adobe Illustrator.

If you'd like to create diagrams that are not specifically based on data, Visio, Gliffy, or OmniGraffle can help by providing predefined shapes and templates for diagrams like flowcharts, org charts, or user interfaces. It can also be useful to create free-form "mind-maps" using tools like MindMeister, TheBrain, or FreeMind that show the relationships between ideas or information in summary format and between parts and wholes. For example, a mind map can be used to represent the objectives and strategies or components of an organization, program, or campaign.

Prezi also provides an interesting, interactive diagramming and presentation tool that allows you to lay out all your information in one large view, and then zoom in and out to focus on different areas.

If you're looking for a more sharable representation of your data, you may consider an infographic, which goes beyond a chart to tell a clear story using data. Infographics have become a popular way to present and share data through social networks like *Facebook, Twitter,* and *Pinterest.* Free tools like infogr.am, Visual.ly, and Easel.ly can help you create your own. Unless you or someone at your organization has considerable experience with design, you may just want to hire a designer.

If you need to display geographic information—from simply plotting addresses on a map to more complex analysis of GPS data—consider *Map and Geographical Information Systems (GIS),* ranging from free tools like Google Maps and Google Earth at the low-end, up to more sophisticated GIS systems like MapWindow or ArcGIS. ●

For more info, visit
www.idealware.org/charts

Collaborating on Diagrams

Want to work together with a group? Gliffy and Google Drive's diagramming tools allow group members to create or update diagrams and flowcharts together in real time over the web. VoiceThread takes on collaboration and commentary in a different way—it allows anyone to make remarks on almost any form of media (including diagrams, charts, drawings, photos, or video) via audio overlay, video popup, or text box.

eAdvocacy

Organizations use a number of online tactics to get constituents involved, like asking them to send emails to decision-makers or politicians, or to take other actions on their behalf. Tools for supporting online actions—often known as *eAdvocacy* tools—make it easier to encourage and manage such techniques.

The software package CitizenSpeak lets you easily create email campaigns for a recipient with a straightforward email address, like a corporate CEO. However, reaching Congressional representatives is more difficult—many block automated emails. You could ask constituents to find and email reps for free through Congress.org, but more expensive tools like Capwiz and a number of Integrated Online Systems (like SalsaLab's Salsa and Blackbaud's Sphere) help supporters draft and send emails that reach the appropriate audience. Change.org and MoveOn also both offer targeted *eAdvocacy* solutions for a fee.

Alternatively, you could ask supporters to write letters to the editor of their local papers. You'll also want to provide contact information for media outlets—again, some more-advanced *Integrated Online Systems* support this. Green Media Tool-shed offers specialized functionality in this area for environmental organizations.

Services have also popped up that aim to replace email as a form of advocacy. Tools like POPVOX let your supporters create profiles, upload their voting history, and directly message their representatives. It's unclear how effective these tools are for advocacy, but as usage increases, they may become as valuable as email. ●

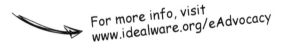

For more info, visit
www.idealware.org/eAdvocacy

Advocacy Through Social Media?

As the popularity of social networking sites has grown, many companies and politicians have joined as well. Consider asking your supporters to make requests on the **Twitter** or **Facebook** accounts of your advocacy targets—if many supporters post, it can provide a public demonstration of the support for your cause. **Twitter** is still the most popular social network for politicians in particular—your supporters might be encouraged to TwitterBomb a legislator with hashtagged content to encourage her to support a certain position, for instance. Act.ly is a free activism site that can target politicians and corporations, and a sister site, GovLuv, lets your supporters find their representatives by street address.

Mobile Apps

An increasing number of your constituents are likely using smartphones or tablet computers. These devices let them browse the web and download mobile applications, or "apps," for more interactive functionality. The easiest ways to reach people through their phones are *Mobile Websites* or *Mobile Text Messaging,* but if you're looking to provide a specific functionality, you might consider creating an app. Apps can engage constituents or provide them with useful information. Staff and volunteers could also use them to carry out organizational work. Unlike a mobile website, which can only be accessed with a Wi-Fi or data connection, apps generally don't need internet access to be useful, but your constituents will need internet access to download them in the first place.

The growing number of competing phones creates a challenge, because apps are platform-dependent—those designed for iPhones won't run on Androids, and vice versa. You need to either make educated assumptions about your users and desired audience, or build multiple apps for competing platforms.

Free apps still dominate the marketplace, but users have shown a willingness to pay a few dollars apiece for apps that manage to be both useful and cool. And that's the challenge—for an app to be popular, it has to be useful. This sounds like common sense, but there's no shortage of businesses creating apps for brand dissemination that don't add any value.

While there are a few tools that allow non-technical users to create very simple mobile apps—like AppMakr, SwebApps, and MobBase—for the most part, creating a mobile app will require a programmer. ●

For more info, visit
www.idealware.org/mobileapps

Mobile Apps for Attendance

Mobile Apps can be a good option for tracking attendance and participation at large, in-person events and trainings due to the availability and portability of mobile phones. There are two types of apps in this area—those that attendees use to "check-in" on their own phones, and those that your staff members can use to take attendance.

Mobile Apps in the first group, like SmartConnect (formerly Geniemobile) from Genie Connect and QuickMobile, allow attendees to check-in, create schedules, and even share notes with other attendees. The downside of these apps, however, is that they require attendees to download them beforehand.

Mobile Apps in the second group, like Event Check-In for Constant Contact, let your staff take attendance on their own phones, either by "checking-in" registrants or scanning QR codes. You could also look at apps designed for teachers, like The Attendance App, Attendance IQ, Attendance, Attendance Tracker, or Meeting Attendance.

Mobile Text Messaging

A huge percentage of adults in the United States—85 percent of them, according to a November 2012 survey by Pew Research Center—have cell phones, making it increasingly desirable for nonprofits to reach out via cell phone text messages, also known as SMS or Short Message Service. Make sure to get their permission before sending them messages, however—the law requires it, and sometimes people need to pay to receive texts.

Texting doesn't have to be expensive. In fact, you can send an email that shows up as a text message by emailing their phone number at their service provider's domain (for example, 2072088172@verizon.net). This isn't officially supported, so isn't likely to work for a large volume, but it's an interesting option to simply reach a few people. Google Voice also lets you send text messages from an online interface. BulkSMS allows you to pay per text message, at about $0.05 per text.

There are a number of online tools that provide more robust services, including the ability to send text messages to targeted sets of subscribers, collect data, provide interactive responses, and manage subscriptions and unsubscribe requests. Vendors, including MobileCause, Mobile Accord/mGive, and Mobile Commons, provide services with interfaces conceptually similar to Broadcast Email tools. MobileCause offers limited functionality starting at $99 per month; the others typically start at about $250 per month.

Most of these services also support mobile giving, which allows subscribers to donate either $5 or $10, added directly to their phone bills. It's not currently possible for them to donate more than $10 at a time, and you'll need to wait until the subscriber pays their phone bill—sometimes as long as several months—to receive the money.

Texting's potential isn't limited to mobile giving, however. Texting works best as a two-way channel. This could be automated using a "branching" set of responses. For example, a supporter who texts "HELP" to a particular number could get information back asking if they're able to help volunteer at an upcoming event. If they answer "YES," they get information about the event in response; if they answer "NO," they might be offered another possible opportunity. A system can also automatically pull responses or information from a database.

In another example, the tool Ushahidi lets you display texts asking for help on a map—in one instance, it was used after the Haiti earthquake to plot areas of greatest need and help locate people close to rescue providers who could be reached quickly. See *Maps and Geographical Information Systems* for more information on how geographic visualization can be useful in program evaluation.

Options like Clickatell or mBlox offer services that allow programmers to automatically send texts from another application or pull text into a database via an application programmer interface. And there are a number of free tools, such as Kannel, Gammu, and FrontlineSMS, which allow you to connect your own cell phone to your computer (or if you need to support a larger number of texts, you could connect a GMS modem to your computer instead of a cell phone) to send bulk text messages. This is a free, robust way to send texts especially in developing countries, but U.S. carriers frown upon the practice, and are likely to shut down your account. ●

For more info, visit
www.idealware.org/text

Get the Code

For people to subscribe to your list, donate, or respond to survey questions via their phones, you'll need an identifying "short code"—many vendors assign you short codes with a keyword specific to your organization. For instance, people might text "SHELTER" to the short code 5634 to subscribe to your list. You can also purchase a custom short code, but at considerable additional expense.

Mobile Websites

More and more people these days are browsing the web with smartphones or tablet computers—almost two-thirds (63 percent) of cell phone owners are using those devices to go online, while around 55 percent of Americans age 18 and older own a tablet, according to two 2013 surveys by Pew Research Center. With the smaller screens found on these devices, websites need to be optimized to be useful. Designing a website to work well on mobile devices isn't as hard as it might sound.

Smartphones will show almost any website, but some look better than others. If you use a phone to look at a website that was designed for typical websites, you will usually see either the upper left hand corner of the website (because that's all that will fit on the small and vertically-oriented phone screen) or a tiny and hard-to-read version of the entire page, shrunk to fit the phone screen. It's worthwhile to consider tweaks to your website to simply make it easier to view on a phone—for instance, consider placing key navigation elements in the top left corner, to allow mobile users to browse without scrolling horizontally, or making navigation elements big enough to be visible even if the whole website shows up in a tiny version on a phone.

The more scalable and strategic way to support mobile devices, however, is building your graphic design using what's called "responsive design." This is a way of coding your website template to rearrange and scale the text, images, and layout of a web page depending on the size of the browser reading it. Your responsive website might appear with three columns and large images on a computer, but only one column and small images on a smartphone. In order to support responsive design, you'll likely need to update the way your graphical design is implemented.

It could be a substantial project to retrofit a responsive design onto an old site—but if you're building a new site, responsive design should definitely be on your list of highly useful features. As a backup strategy, if you need substantial mobile support but a responsive design isn't practical, you could also consider creating a second, simplified site streamlined for mobile phones. Free of animation or design elements that might not work on phones, this site would be a pared-down version of your regular site that scrolls vertically. (For an example, compare http://m. ebay.com to www.ebay.com.) Updating the content on both a regular and a mobile site will require double entry, in most cases, so this is more of a stopgap than a long-term solution. ●

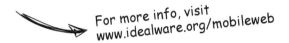

For more info, visit
www.idealware.org/mobileweb

Online Advertising

Online Advertising lets you advertise your organization or mission through other people's websites. Some sites limit you to text ads, while others let you run banner ads—usually an image limited to a particular size, though animation and interactive banner ads are sometimes possible. You typically pay for ads by "impression"—the number of times the ad shows on a site—or by "click"—the number of times any user clicks on the ad.

Google AdWords are a common, cost-effective method. You create a short text ad and choose the keywords and geographic area you'd like to reach, and Google posts your ad next to searches for them. Google provides easy-to-use tools to track your results and further optimize campaigns, making it straightforward to manage. Cost depends on the popularity of the keywords you choose, but often starts at just a few cents for each user who clicks through to your site—and you can cap the amount you spend per day. Even better, qualifying nonprofits can get a huge number of free ads per month through the Google Grants program.

Social Networking Sites, specifically *Facebook* and *LinkedIn,* also support online ads similar to Google's, usually for a similar price. Advertisers have the option to create either text- or image-based ads, and pay either per click or per impression. They also let you target a number of different demographics. Facebook charges a $1 per day minimum in the U.S., and has also introduced the ability to boost certain posts so that more of your Facebook fans see them in their newsfeed. *Twitter* also has launched an ad program.

Many *Blogs* and websites also accept ads, a good way to target a particular niche audience. Companies like Blogads facilitate advertising across a number of different sites. These networks typically let you search for *Blogs* and websites by demographic, audience size, and prices. Prices vary greatly depending on the blog, placement, and duration, but start as low as $10 per site per week for less-known sites. ●

For more info, visit
www.idealware.org/ads

Podcasts

Podcasts are syndicated audio or video shows that allow people to subscribe. When a new show is available, files are automatically downloaded onto subscribers' computers. In fact, that's the main difference between *Podcasts* and other types of audio or video files—Podcasts are subscription-based and downloaded via *RSS*, so subscribers don't have to seek them out. *Podcasts* were all the rage a few years ago, but their popularity has waned somewhat.

Nonprofits can use them in a number of ways to create awareness or educate people about their causes. *Podcasts* can be useful to record and broadcast meetings, conference calls, speeches, and more. Keep in mind, though, that creating polished multimedia content is time-consuming. If you have the audio or visual content or the experience to create *Podcasts*, they can provide an interesting way to distribute information, but think carefully about the time involved before committing yourself to creating new multimedia content on a regular basis.

The first step is to record audio or video using a microphone or camera, and edit it using *Multimedia Editing Software*. Once you've polished the content and exported it into a standard file format, decide whether to post the *Podcast* on your own site or on a site designed to store them, like Hipcast.com, libsyn, Podbus, Ourmedia, or others. These sites range from free to around $200 per month.

Once your *Podcast* is hosted and published, people can subscribe via most *RSS* readers. You should also submit your podcast to a site like iTunes that allows people to easily find it. On these sites, users search for *Podcasts* or enter their web addresses, and the site downloads the files directly onto their computers or iPods as soon as they are available. ●

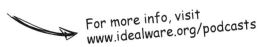

For more info, visit
www.idealware.org/podcasts

QR Codes

A *QR code* is a square bar code very similar in concept to the grocery store checkout codes you find on everything from bunches of bananas to cans of beans. Unlike those codes, though, you can scan a *QR code* using the camera on your smartphone to be automatically directed to a particular web address. This will work with most smartphones, though for some you'll need to download an application (usually free) to enable it.

Where might nonprofits use them? For example, you could add them to your newsletter and have them easily route people to a webpage where they can sign up for your eNewsletter, instead. Or include one on a direct mail piece to provide easy access to your online donation functionality. They cost nothing but the space on the page to print them. *QR codes* have been especially useful for museums, zoos and animal parks, and other educational organizations that want to include additional information related to their exhibits.

Of course, your constituents will need to have a smartphone to use them, as well as some idea what the *QR codes* are—and what to do with them. For most nonprofits, experience has shown that the codes are only likely to reach a small segment of the population. ●

For more info, visit
www.idealware.org/qrcodes

Search Engine Optimization

Search Engine Optimization (SEO) isn't a type of software but a set of techniques to help search engines like Google or Bing find your website and show it high up on the list of results people see when they search for terms you specify.

Two steps in particular make a big difference. First, encourage as many sites as possible to link to you. These links help search engines find your site, and the more incoming links from credible organizations, the higher you're listed in search results. Second, identify keywords for which you'd like to be found, and use them prominently—for instance, to be found by those searching for "food pantries in Cincinnati," use the words "food," "pantry," and "Cincinnati" often in page text, prominent headers, titles, and even page file names.

A good *Web Content Management System* can help place your keywords effectively, as well as help with the more technical aspects of SEO. *Website Analytics* tools can then help you track the keywords used to find your site.

It's often useful to go beyond SEO and consider paid placement, as well. For example, some search engines let you buy ads for particular search terms (this technique, called Search Engine Marketing, is covered in the *Online Advertising* section). In particular, Google offers a Google Grants program that provides free Google Ads to qualifying nonprofits. ●

For more info, visit
www.idealware.org/seo

Web Content Management Systems

Web Content Management Systems (CMS) let you create and maintain customized websites, update their graphic design and navigation over time, take advantage of contributed modules, and automate routine updates—for instance, removing events from your homepage after they've come and gone. Most won't let you update existing sites built in other systems, however; if you want to implement a CMS for an existing site, you will have to rebuild, and sometimes redesign, the site. Their real benefit is the ability to update site content and navigation without technical know-how or web design experience. Many organizations hire consultants to build the initial site in a CMS, and then use the system to maintain it.

Widely used open source options include WordPress, Joomla, Drupal, and Plone. These systems are free to download, but you'll need someone with technical skills to set them up. Other systems, like Ektron, CommonSpot by PaperThin, Sitecore, and CrownPeak, provide sophisticated CMS functionality starting at about $10,000 for the first year. Some systems, like eZ Publish, Evoq (formerly DotNetNuke), and ExpressionEngine, offer the flexibility of an open source system at a low licensing fee, or offer both a paid enterprise-level and free community versions. For more straightforward sites, consider simple tools like Wix, Weebly, or Squarespace that let you define navigation, pick a graphic design template, and enter text and images on simple web-based forms.

Larger nonprofits looking for both enterprise-level function-ality and strong integration with constituent management may want to look into Blackbaud's NetCommunity or Luminate CMS (formerly Convio). Some *Integrated Online Systems* may also provide CMS functionality in addition to such features as constituent management and *Broadcast Email* functionality. ●

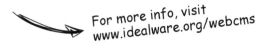

For more info, visit
www.idealware.org/webcms

What About Updating Existing Sites?

Other desktop tools, like Adobe Contribute or Adobe Dreamweaver, also let less-technical people update websites, but they work by directly changing the code for individual pages. These are the only tools that will help update existing sites—however, they limit your ability to make updates that are more substantial or affect multiple pages. CMS systems are the better approach if you're building a site from scratch.

To build your base, once you've found new supporters you need to continue to communicate with them over time to deepen your relationships. From Petitions and Pledges to Twitter and other Social Networking Sites, there have never been more ways to engage your constituents in ongoing conversations.

All of the software names highlighted within the text are covered in more detail in this guide. Most of them are included in this section, and follow immediately after the descriptions. If you're interested in a software type and can't find it in this section, you can look it up in the Index.

The right software can help you grow your relationships with supporters and encourage them to help your organization in more important ways.

....

Strongly consider...

Newsletters can keep supporters in the loop on your organization's issues and actions. Many organizations now offer eNewsletters in addition to, or instead of, print newsletters, but print newsletters continue to be traditional and effective, if expensive to print. *Page Layout* tools can help you create professional-looking templates that substantially ease the process of publishing each new issue. Learn about that technology in our Back Office and Productivity section. If you're sending out an eNewsletter, *Broadcast Email* software helps you manage your list of subscribers, create your emails, and view reports on their success—we cover that tool in One-Way Communications.

Whether online or off, photographs can be a terrific way to make your activities come alive. Digital cameras and smartphones make taking photos easy, but you'll want *Photo Editing* software (discussed in Back Office and Productivity) to help prepare them for print or the web. *Photo Sharing Websites* can also ease the process of distributing them to an audience over the web, but they're being largely overtaken by *Facebook, Twitter,* Tumblr, and other new sites.

Get your supporters talking—with you, with each other, or both. *Email Discussion Lists* foster email conversations, while *Facebook, Twitter,* and *Niche Social Networking Sites* are other ways for supporters to stay in touch. *LinkedIn* can not only help you meet new people—including volunteers, board members, constituents, and other like-minded people—but offers some interesting possibilities for discussions. *Social Media Measuring* refers to the process and tools you use to track the success of your efforts; it also lets you adapt and adjust what you're doing to better achieve your goals—learn more in our Listening and Measuring section.

Keeping ahead of the curve...

The more frequently you can tell your story online, the better. *Blogs* provide useful forums for staff members, volunteers, or those in the field to keep supporters in the loop about your organization's work. *RSS* (covered in our Listening and Measuring section) can let supporters subscribe to your online content. Multimedia stories can be particularly compelling, if you have the time and skills to create them—*Multimedia Editing* tools, discussed in Back Office and Productivity, help you create professional, compelling materials. *Video Sharing Websites* can help you share videos.

Don't underestimate the usefulness of engaging supporters by asking them to take action. Consider creating a *Petition* or *Pledge* on your organization's behalf.

On the cutting edge...

If you already have a strong community, online tools can help you deepen and facilitate conversations. Consider *Custom Online Communities* to support your private community, or Wikis (covered in Collaboration) to collaboratively build a website together with those who share your organization's cause or interests. Another way to leverage a particularly engaged constituent base is *Crowdsourcing* for information or expertise. *Social Content Websites* can help you promote your cause as well. ●

Blogs

Blogs are websites where you post commentary, stories, links, or even photos, videos, audio files, or maps—often in a personal voice. Posts are shown in order by date, starting with the most recent. Subscribers can comment on what you've written, helping you to interact with your constituents and hear what's important to them.

Blogs can be an interesting way to show your organization's expertise and human side, but they only work if you're able to post regularly. It takes quite a bit of effort to keep blogs fresh, and it's obvious when you aren't posting, so make sure you're able to devote the time and effort to keep it going.

A number of software packages make creating and updating blogs quick and easy, even for non-technical users. Many *Web Content Management Systems* offer some blogging functionality—if you're using one to update your website, it almost certainly makes sense to start there in thinking about supporting a new blog. If you need to look further, Blogger, WordPress.com, and Typepad are all commonly used and very affordable. Tumblr is a free and customizable option, but you cannot host it on your organization's website. WordPress.org and ExpressionEngine offer more-advanced functionality for those with more technical expertise.

All of these tools let you set up a blog, customize its appearance, add links to important actions like donating or signing up for a newsletter, and then post text, photos, or videos. All support reader comments and let you moderate comments for inappropriate content or spam. These tools also let readers subscribe to your blog via *RSS* tools—an important functionality, since some people read blogs solely via *RSS*.

Most tools also support multiple bloggers, which can help share the expertise of your staff or volunteers and help keep the blog fresh and interesting. More sophisticated blog tools like WordPress.org and Movable Type, and *Web Content Management Systems* like Drupal, let you manage complex blogging workflows—for instance, setting a central administrator who approves posts written by multiple bloggers—or integrate blog posts into larger websites in sophisticated ways. ●

For more info, visit www.idealware.org/blogs

Crowdsourcing

Crowdsourcing is less a technology than a strategy for enlisting help or answers from the internet. Unlike the similarly named "outsourcing," *Crowdsourcing* relies on the assistance and expertise of the broader internet audience (the "crowd") rather than a specific individual. The process has a long history, from humble beginnings as a general open-call for help on discussion boards, but in recent years social media and new technologies have made it easier for organizations to reach and engage broader audiences.

Nonprofits have used *Crowdsourcing* for everything from marketing and fundraising to volunteerism and activism. It's a great way to enlist help from a wider community knowledgebase, and to engage people in your work.

If you're trying to pool collective knowledge on a specific question or subject, the open-call technique still works, whether through social networks like *Facebook, Twitter,* or *LinkedIn, Email Discussion Lists,* or through specific crowdsourcing platforms, like Ushahidi for collecting geographic data on certain types of incidents.

If you're trying to do a specific task instead of just collecting information or answers, you can also turn to the crowd for micro-volunteering, where people can spend a short amount of time performing a small task, from translating text into other languages, data entry, or even tagging photos. Different platforms exist for specific tasks, like Lingotek for translation, while other online tools like Sparked or Amazon's Mechanical Turk can work for a broader range of tasks. You might also explore *Crowdfunding* tools like Kickstarter or Indiegogo, or microfinance sites like Kiva.

Overall, *Crowdsourcing* will be more effective if you make it very clear what you want the crowd to do, break down your strategic goals into smaller tasks people can help with, engage the crowd and reward participation, and stay positive. ●

For more resources, visit
www.idealware.org/crowdsourcing

Custom Online Communities

Want to provide a way for committed constituents to connect with each other for discussions and to share information? It likely makes sense to dip your toe in the water of an *Email Discussion List* or group through an existing platform, like *Facebook* or *LinkedIn*. If you have a lot of active community members, however, a *Custom Online Community* allows you somewhat more in the way of features and customization.

One approach is to use a custom social network tool. These packages let you create a network site from a template, customize the site's look and feel, and choose features and functionality—including discussion boards and email options, events and calendars, and libraries of documents, videos, and pictures. Members create profiles to view, post, or interact with the site. Ning and Groupsite offer free, ad-supported custom social network software, or inexpensive ad-free options. More tech-savvy organizations should also consider the KIT Digital (formerly KickApps) or Elgg, a powerful, free, and open source software package you download and host on your own web server.

If your members are already familiar with each other, *Project Management Software* like Basecamp or Central Desktop or collaborative document services like Google Drive allow for straightforward file sharing and the ability to host shared conversations. Other options include Wikis or online discussion forums (also called bulletin boards) supported through tools like vBulletin and phpBB.

Whatever method you use, there are a few things to keep in mind. *Custom Online Communities* take a lot of effort to develop and maintain—are your constituents really going to be eager to join yet another online community? Can you afford the staff time to seed and grow your community? And with so many popular social networks available, do you really need to start one? Make sure you have an audience ready and eager to interact with each other in your new online community. ●

For more info, visit
www.idealware.org/communities

Email Discussion Lists

Email Discussion Lists, often called "listservs" for the original software application that supported them, let people subscribe to topic- or group-oriented discussions. When a subscriber emails a specific automated address, the message is emailed out to all of the list's subscribers. Other subscribers respond, and an ongoing discussion unfolds in inboxes. As email is familiar to a wide audience, email discussion lists can be a straightforward way to encourage people to talk to each other online.

Most of these tools let people subscribe or unsubscribe, decide whether to receive messages as they're sent or in digest form to cut down on emails, and choose to view messages either via email or in a web interface. Most let users search archives online. Administrators can moderate emails, and more advanced tools let you customize the graphic design of the interface and more easily integrate the email addresses with your other databases.

Both Google Groups and Yahoo! Groups offer basic discussion list functionality for free, but include prominent ads in the email messages. Electric Ember's NPOGroups offers similar functionality without the ads, and Groupsite adds a bit more power for a little more cost. GoLightly is more expensive, but very versatile, and offers such additional functionality as Blogs, Wikis, libraries, and video. LSoft is a high-end and customizable solution that lets you have a listserv with your own domain name. ●

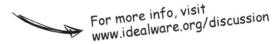
For more info, visit
www.idealware.org/discussion

Do You Already Have a Tool?

Integrated Online Systems, Constituent Relationship Management, and **Website Content Management Systems** often include email discussion list capabilities. Your web hosting providers may offer Mailman, a basic discussion list package, for free. Both Custom Online Communities and Social Networking Sites can also provide some of this functionality (LinkedIn Groups is a particularly strong option), though they tend to support online conversations better than they do email discussions.

Facebook

Facebook is the largest Social Networking Site. With more than one billion users worldwide, it's taken root in a way that's made it nearly impossible to ignore.

You create a page for your organization and invite current or potential constituents to "like" your Page. You can then promote events, host discussions, or solicit donations there. Your updated information is likely to be seen not only by the people who directly "like" your page but by some of their friends, as well, allowing new people to find out about your organization without substantial effort. Most organizations will find it useful to create at least a basic page with their name and contact information.

You can also target updates geographically or according to language or demographic criteria. For example, you could publish a message that would only be seen by your male, Spanish-speaking followers in the U.S., and *Facebook's* Graph Search provides even more specific search functionality.

Facebook can foster discussion and get people talking to each other and to your organization. The site provides an interesting way for organizations to keep people up to date on events, cause-related information, and news links, and can offer a means of sharing videos and photos as well. It can also be useful for marketing events and gatherings, and when people RSVP online, their friends can see it, helping to spread the word. A *Facebook* Group, unlike a Page, provides a closed community for members, which can be a useful way to comply with privacy or confidentiality guidelines, or simply provide a safe place for your constituents to interact with each other. *Facebook* also offers ads, which can be targeted to reach a very specific audience (for more, see *Online Advertising*).

There are a number of apps that can expand the functionality of a nonprofit's *Facebook* Page. For instance, most *Broadcast Email* tools provide you with an app to build your email list on Facebook, and marketing services like Tradable Bits let you drive campaigns to your supporters.

With *Facebook,* as with all social media, results will vary widely among different organizations. You should consider your audience and your mission, as well as how much time you'll be able to invest, when creating a social media strategy. ●

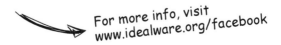

For more info, visit
www.idealware.org/facebook

Geolocation Applications

If your organization has a public physical location, like a museum, or does a lot of on-site advocacy or volunteer events, *Geolocation Applications* can be an interesting way to engage constituents. These social networking applications track users' physical locations—often using the GPS chip in their smart-phones—and lets them "check-in" to places to let others in their network know where they are.

With Foursquare, for instance, you enter your organization's venue into the application and people "check-in" via their phone when they arrive. Foursquare then tells your friends where you are, spreading the word via their app on Twitter or Face-book. The person who checks into your venue most frequently becomes known as the "mayor" of that venue, providing addi-tional incentive for people to check in. Additional possible uses include offering discounts to the current mayor or to all who check-in during a specific time frame or showing photos on your website of everyone who checks in. Or you could treat users who check-in frequently as super-activists and engage them to spread the word further.

Foursquare was the early leader in this area, but it's not alone. *Facebook's* check-in functionality is part of status updates and the newer review functionality. Google+ also lets you share loca-tion. Yelp, Around Me, and Loopt work in similar ways.

Regardless of the application, the hope is that getting people to check in could boost attendance and awareness of your location among their friends, increasing your own audience.

There's a lot of public conversation about the privacy issues posed by applications that reveal location, but such concerns have much more important implications for individuals than for organizations. ●

For more info, visit
www.idealware.org/geolocate

Creating a Mobile "Field Trip"

A newer use of geolocation includes apps that guide users on walking "field trips," to either guide users on a programmed tour of nearby locations, or simply alert users when they are near something of interest. For example, Movable Feast allows users to tie multimedia to points on a map, creating a tour as engaging remotely as it is in person. It works through Google Maps, where a tour taker can look at photos, videos, audio, or text added to a particular location to learn more about it. This functionality may be particularly suited for cultural heritage organizations, museums, and historical societies.

Other organizations might want to consider adding information to Google Field Trip. Smartphone users can log into the application and be notified when they are near something of interest. The notification will take them to photos of the location and provide information about it. Google Field Trip is less intimate and personalized than Movable Feast, since you can't tailor a user's experience or share audio and video, but people using Field Trip are more likely to stumble across your content since Movable Feast requires users to seek out tours and download them.

LinkedIn

With more than 250 million members, *LinkedIn* is an interesting site that falls somewhere between social networking for the general public and a *Niche Social Networking* site for professionals. A *LinkedIn* profile is essentially a resume. People describe their work history and skills, and can include educational background, references, associations, and more. Each person can link their profile to other people they know—when you link to people, you see their profiles and all of their contacts. *LinkedIn* has two sides: it's both a useful place to search networks to find potential contacts and new friends, and also has interesting potential to support groups related to professional networking.

LinkedIn provides an interesting way to look for connections to people your organization might want to meet. If you're looking for new donors, staff members, volunteers, or board members, especially those with specific skill sets, consider *LinkedIn* as a research and recruiting tool. You'll need to set up a company profile for your organization first—it's free. The interface makes it easy to search on who in your network might know a major donor or a staff member at a local bank or foundation that you'd like to approach. *LinkedIn* also offers recruiting solutions, and has now started discounting them somewhat for nonprofits.

LinkedIn is likely to be of particular interest to groups whose mission is to support people in their jobs or who have a focus on careers. As an organization, you can create a *LinkedIn* group for people to join. Members can hold discussions, post resources of interest, or create a job board. Group members also receive digest emails of the discussions and postings—as an organization, you can select what content is included in these emails. ●

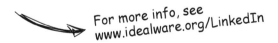

For more info, see
www.idealware.org/LinkedIn

Niche Social Networking Sites

Want to provide a way for committed constituents to connect? Social networking websites are free online communities where supporters can easily keep up to date on your organization and, in most cases, "talk" with you and other supporters. The most popular are *Facebook* and *Twitter,* but there are many others which tend to be more niche-oriented, focusing on particular groups with a specific set of interests and identities. This is how they compete on the market—and exactly why they may be useful to your organization.

There are hundreds of more specifically targeted niche social networks to choose from—here are a few by interest:

- Care2 and Wiser.org. Aimed at users who value social and environmental causes.

- DeHood and Blasterous. For networking with your specific neighborhood or local community.

- Qzone, Netlog, and Orkut. Popular international social networks (for China, Europe, and Brazil, respectively).

- Tumblr. A photo-heavy and streamlined blogging platform (read more in our *Blogs* section).

- Reddit. Where users submit links of the most interesting content on the web and others can then choose to "upvote" or "downvote" the content to determine how much priority the link is given (also covered in our *Social Content Websites* section).

In addition, due to marketing or changing demographics, social networks originally designed or intended for general audiences may find themselves becoming niche sites. Two good examples of general networks that became niche are MySpace and Google+.

MySpace was designed to be of general interest, similar to Facebook, and the two were equally popular several years ago, but MySpace has seen a substantial decline. However, MySpace has recently been sold and re-launched as a niche site with a focus on music. Google+, on the other hand, was launched a few years ago as Google's answer to Facebook, and brought several intriguing new features, like the Hangouts video chat rooms, as well as more control over privacy and sharing settings. However, Google+ has not built the audience that Facebook did. It did manage to build a following in the technology community, especially among digital photographers, and could today be considered a Niche Social Network—although once again, Google+ is surging in popularity, and is worth keeping in sights as a mainstream option for the future. ●

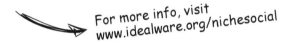

For more info, visit www.idealware.org/nichesocial

Petitions and Pledges

People sign their names and other contact information to online petitions, which are sent to an organization or a person, like a government agency or Congressman, to show that large groups of people support a particular cause or viewpoint. Online pledges are similar, but signers typically pledge to take a particular action—for instance, to stop drinking bottled water—and the list of pledges isn't necessarily sent to anyone.

Nonprofits often use both as list-building tools to gather contact information from those interested in their causes.

Technical components of *Pledges* and *Petitions* are the same—you need a web page with information, a way for "signers" to submit their contact information, and a way for your organization to see the contact information of those who signed the petition or pledge. It's also useful to be able to customize the look and feel of the page, or add your logo.

Since the basic functionality is a simple online form, you may already have software that can help. For instance, most *Web Content Management Systems* let you create web forms. Some *Integrated Online, Donor Management,* and *Constituent Relationship Management Systems* provide similar functionality, and flow information about those who sign directly into your constituent database. Simple online form builders, like Google Forms, Wufoo, or Formstack, could also be used for basic *Petitions* and *Pledges.*

Quite a few sites provide specific functionality to support nonprofit petitions or pledges, including Care2's ThePetitionSite, Change.org, MoveOn.org's Petitions, PledgeBank, and Causes. Even the White House now offers We the People, a site on which any American citizen can browse and support petitions, or create their own. These sites allow you to promote your cause to their existing audiences, and sometimes provide more sophisticated functionality, like the easy ability to show the names or total number of people who have signed. Make sure it's easy to export contact information for those who've signed—some tools make it difficult, or charge additional fees. ●

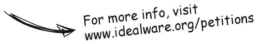 For more info, visit www.idealware.org/petitions

Photo Sharing Websites

Photo Sharing Websites let you post photos in a central location where staff, constituents, or anyone else can see them. You can upload your photos to these free sites, organize them, and perform minor editing—for instance, cropping, correcting colors, or removing red-eye. (For more serious manipulation, use *Photo Editing Software*.) Many social media sites have incorporated photo sharing in a big way. *Facebook* is a very popular way to share photos, adding valuable content to your organization's page, and, with its acquisition of Instagram, taps into that tool's existing community. Instagram itself might also be worth considering, especially for organizations who work a lot with young people. Flickr, Picasa, Snapfish, and Photobucket are also widely used. These sites let anyone easily post their photos. They're not only good for letting your constituents see pictures, but also for letting them post their own pictures of your events or organization. It's easy to tag pictures in order to easily collect them in a group. Not all your supporters will want their picture online, however—be sure to get permission before posting or tagging photos from your events, especially if there are children involved.

These sites can be useful to share photos across an organization, as well. Because they're online, remote staff can easily access them, and they're backed up in case of a fire or hard drive crash. However, these tools don't offer particularly robust functionality to organize or search if you have hundreds or thousands of photos—*Digital Asset Management* software could be helpful for these more sophisticated needs. ●

 For more info, visit
www.idealware.org/photosharing

Photo Sharing Meets Social Networking

All the sites listed here also offer social networking features to broaden the number of people who will see your photos. For example, Flickr lets you invite people to join your group to easily see your most recent pictures—they can comment, add keywords, or tag people in photos, making it more likely that people interested in your subject will find them. And Pinterest lets your friends "re-pin" your photos to their own boards.

Social Content Websites

More and more nonprofits are taking advantage of the popularity of websites where readers help create the content. These sites can provide interesting opportunities to promote your cause by distributing your articles or resources to a broad online audience.

For example, you could help people find your articles or resources by adding them, with keywords, onto "social bookmarking" sites where people share links, like Delicious.com. Or you can promote your content on "social news" sites like Digg and Reddit—you add articles or links that readers can vote on, and popularity determines how prominently the link is shown. Pinterest also lets you sort and post links and images to an online pinboard—it's popular for organizations that do social marketing.

Alternatively, you could promote your whole organization through nonprofit specific "charity portals" such as GreatNonprofits.org, Good.is, GlobalGiving.org, or Change.org. These sites allow you to post information or a profile about your organization to try to reach those interested in your cause.

You might also help shape the conversation about your organization and issues on Wikipedia, a publicly maintained encyclopedia, where readers add or edit almost any entry on the vast site. It's important to avoid appearing biased or self-promotional—entries are watched closely, and other editors will remove what they don't find useful. ●

For more info, visit
www.idealware.org/socialcontent

Are They Already Talking About Your Issue?

It's likely there are at least a few existing communities—forums, **Blogs, Email Discussion Lists, Social Networks,** or shared calendars—where people are already talking about the issues you care about. Participating is an easy, effective way to understand what your constituents care about, promote your organization, and reach new supporters. But how do you find these communities? You can search the web with **Online Listening** tools to find conversations about your issue. Or ask your volunteers, board members, or constituents to scan places they go online.

Twitter

Twitter is a popular social networking system that lets you create a minimal profile for your organization, and send out a stream of short messages called "tweets"—updates about what you're doing, conversation starters, requests for help, or links to resources of interest. Tweets are limited to 140 characters or less.

You can use the Twitter.com website to manage your account, but many people instead choose to tweet via applications like Tweet-Deck or HootSuite that allow much more sophisticated management of incoming and outgoing tweets—both on smartphones and computer desktops.

People can choose to "follow" your *Twitter* account, which is like subscribing to your feed, and if they particularly like one of your tweets they can "retweet" it, or post it again so their own followers see it. It's in retweeting that much of the power of *Twitter* lies. If you post something interesting that's retweeted exponentially, you can reach a huge amount of people very quickly.

You can also use "hashtags" (the # symbol, sometimes known as the "hash," followed by a one-word keyword) to post a tweet to a certain group. For instance, including the #nptech tag will flag your post as relating to nonprofit technology and make it more likely to be seen by those following #nptech tweets. The # symbol makes your keyword or phrase easily searchable by others—various sites even track existing hashtags you can search before creating your own.

Many individuals and organizations also use URL shorteners like Bit.ly, Ow.ly, or TinyURL to convert long web addresses into more space-friendly short ones.

With all social media, results will vary widely among different organizations. *Twitter* users tend to be more tech-savvy. You should consider your audience and your mission, as well as how much time you'll be able to invest, before assuming that *Twitter* makes sense for you. ●

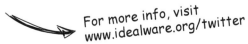

For more info, visit
www.idealware.org/twitter

Video Sharing and Streaming

Videos can provide a compelling way to tell your story online. While professional looking video can be expensive to produce, both in staff time and actual money, video-sharing websites let you upload videos to the web for free. Once they're online, viewers can comment and share them with friends. In general, you maintain ownership of the videos you post, but you grant the site certain rights. Before you post a video, read the site's Policies and Terms carefully.

There are many free video-sharing options, including YouTube, Blip, and Vimeo. Daily DoGooder is geared specifically at nonprofits. Brightcove lets you show videos and video pages without any logo or branding for Brightcove itself, but starts at $99 per month. YouTube offers nonprofit-specific functionality, like the ability to create a branded YouTube channel, link calls-to-action directly in videos, or accept donations directly through the video page.

It's also straightforward to broadcast video to the web live. Services like UStream allow you to record videos via a photo or digital video camera and transmit them live on the web.

Many of these *Video Sharing Websites* also allow you to post the videos on your own web page or blog. They provide HTML (the coding language of websites) for you to copy and paste to embed the video. In most cases, the sites' logos are displayed on these videos.

There are also applications which allow you to create sharable videos right from your smartphone. Vine (for Twitter), Instagram Video, Cinemagram, and GifBoom offer tools to create, edit, and share short, simple video clips. While these applications have their limitations, they can be powerful tools for expressing a brief message that couldn't be easily communicated with a photograph. ●

Want to "Go Viral?"

If enough people share a video, it can spread around the web exponentially, eventually reaching an enormous audience. This rare, sought-after phenomenon is known as "going viral." There's no recipe for creating viral videos, but you can start by making sure it's relevant and irresistible enough to compel people to share. And then cross your fingers.

For more info, visit
www.idealware.org/videosharing

To put technology to use for your organization, you'll need to choose the right tool and implement it—often a daunting process. Complex software can be expensive, and implementation can be difficult. You also need to plan for training and supporting staff and moving your data to the new system.

By following the steps outlined in this section, you can navigate this process successfully, remove the frustration, and minimize the risk.

It's not enough to know what kinds of software might work for you. You also need to carefully think through how to find the right software for your needs, and how to get it up and running smoothly.

• •

Regardless of the type of software you're considering, the first critical step is *Defining Your Software Needs*. For a minor purchase, this step might involve a quick conversation with other staff, but for a large, mission-critical piece of software, it might take months of work. Before you go any further, make sure you don't already have a system that will do what you need. Can you expand an existing system to take on more functionality? Making use of existing systems means saving the time, money, and frustration of choosing, installing, and learning a whole new application.

If you do need new software, the next step is *Creating a Software Shortlist* to winnow down all the possible options to a manageable list. For a minor purchase, this might mean simply talking to a few people and choosing a single package to explore further, but if you're making more of an investment, you'll want to investigate more in-depth and identify a list of three-to-five software options.

The next step is *Evaluating Software*—you wouldn't buy a car without test-driving it, would you? Try out each system on your own, or ask the vendors to demo them for you. Make sure to evaluate them for the real world scenarios for which you'll use them and not just a hypothetical list of features.

As you're considering different options, you may find yourself *Comparing Open Source and Proprietary Software,* or *Comparing Installed and Cloud-Based Software.* There are pros and cons to each of these different types, but what matters most at the end of the day is the ability of the tool you choose to meet your needs and the cost of the system both upfront and over time. *Evaluating the Software Contract* is critical to making sure you know what you would be purchasing—especially for more complicated software.

If you're choosing a complex, mission-critical component, consider hiring a consultant who knows the market and can help define your needs. *Choosing a Consultant* doesn't have to be scary—think of it as a way to add valuable outside experience to your team.

Once you've chosen your software, you're only about half-done—you still need to implement it. Depending on the type of system you've chosen, you may need to think about *Migrating Data,* or moving it from your old systems into your new one. This is rarely an easy step, and it requires careful consideration and planning. In addition, no matter how amazing your new system is, it's useless to you if no one knows how to use it—however big or small your new system is, make sure you plan for *Training and Supporting Staff.* Who should they turn to with questions? What should they do, or not do, with the system?

Finally, no system will maintain itself—particularly one that includes data. *Caring for Your Data* means establishing policies to ensure your data stays clean and actionable, and that it's easy to access the information you need from the system. The best way to keep data useful is to do so right from the start: What should staff think about when entering records? Who will monitor data quality? Help your staff know what they should enter and when, and define the steps that will ensure your data is clean and usable when someone tries to find something. ●

How can a nonprofit most effectively implement software? We've provided an example of how a fictional-but-realistic organization used best practices to introduce new technologies. All of the processes highlighted within the text are covered in more detail in the next section.

....

StreamWatch
Putting Technology Into Place

$250,000 Budget

StreamWatch is a small, expanding organization with a mission to protect, conserve, and monitor runs of wild sea-run fish in Oregon's coastal rivers. Until now, the staff has used Excel for everything from donor-tracking and budgeting to human resources. Nick, the executive director, decided the organization has outgrown the tool, and applied for and received a grant to cover the cost of a database—the largest single purchase in the organization's history.

To begin with, Nick sat down with the staff for a conversation about *Defining Software Needs* and identifying the many goals they wanted the new software to accomplish: tracking donors and the army of volunteers that carry out the nonprofit's field work, coordinating broadcast emails and the quarterly newsletter to keep constituents up-to-speed on conservation issues and relevant legislation, and managing the fundraising events and galas that support both the staff and the mission. While this process immediately yielded a long list of "must-have" features, subsequent meetings culled the list to those features most necessary to the organization's day-to-day functions and an additional list of desirable "nice-to-haves" that were not deal-breakers.

Since StreamWatch would be working with a system for the first time, Nick asked around at other nonprofits about *Choosing a Consultant* to help the staff understand and streamline their processes, and hired someone to make sure they were getting off on the right foot. The consultant talked Nick through the various options, including *Comparing Open Source and Proprietary Software* and *Comparing Installed and Cloud-Based Software,* and helped *Create a Software Shortlist* by identifying the most-common software tools used by other nonprofits with similar needs. Based on her own experience, she made recommendations about which might be a good fit for StreamWatch. Of her list of five, two were out of reach financially, leaving a final list of three.

Nick scheduled vendor demos to facilitate *Evaluating the Software* on the list, and sat down with the consultant and the key staff members who would be using the system. Most of the systems more than met the nonprofit's needs—both current and anticipated as it continues to grow—but the demos made it very clear that one system was substantially more-user friendly for what they needed to do. Nick worked with the vendor to negotiate terms, asked the organization's attorney to *Evaluate the Software Contract,* and made the purchase.

The next two months passed quickly. Because all the organization's data was spread out across a number of Excel workbooks, staff worked with the vendor and consultant on *Migrating Data* into the new database to make sure it was consolidated and secure. The vendor also worked toward *Training and Supporting Staff* on using the system and *Caring for Data,* including teaching them the best data-entry and recordkeeping practices to ensure that StreamWatch would get the full value of what the new software could bring to the organization. ●

Defining Your Software Needs

Before you invest in new software, first determine exactly what you need. If you're buying just an inexpensive piece of software for one person, defining your needs can be a quick process, but if you're buying a major piece of software, itemizing your requirements will require a serious commitment—and perhaps take a month or more.

It's critical to consult with your staff and representatives of anyone who will use the system about their desires, critical needs, and frustrations. Make a list of what will be useful to your organization. If you define more than a dozen or so needs, prioritize them—what's critical, and what's just nice to have? If a requirement is critical, that means you would discard a system from your list simply for not meeting it. When you don't prioritize your requirements, it's all too easy to hold out for a system that's ideal in every way—which isn't something you're likely to actually find, or afford on your budget.

Once you have a list of requirements, evaluate your current system against that list to make sure it truly won't work to meet your critical needs. It's worth calling the vendor to ask—you might not be aware of all the processes your current system is capable of. Switching systems often requires substantial time and cost in selecting, moving data, and training, so make sure you aren't wasting resources replacing software that would actually work fine for your needs. Investing in better training is often more cost-effective than switching entirely.

If you are having trouble understanding how a system can best help your organization, consider hiring a consultant who can help you see how your organization handles data, and offer solutions that have worked for other clients in similar situations. When the time comes to work with vendors and find the right software, you will be glad you can understand and explain your organization's needs with confidence. ●

For more information, visit www.idealware.org/definingneeds

Creating a Software Shortlist

There sheer number of software companies out there will make your head spin. Some initial research can narrow down your list of choices to a more manageable size and allow you to conduct a reasonable comparison of vendors and systems.

Start by seeing if credible sources have already provided a vendor roundup as a starting point. Idealware, NTEN, and TechSoup are all good places to get started, and organizations that support your particular sector—for instance, an association of nonprofits with a focus in your area—might also have useful resources.

Speak with other organizations about what software they're using and the overall effectiveness of their systems. This will give you a general overview of some of the big-name software you should be considering as well as perspective on how software can help your organization. Keep your needs in mind, and you should be well on your way to making an informed decision.

If you're only making a minor software purchase, it may be sufficient to identify one or two tools that seem like they will work. For a larger investment, create a list of three to six tools for deeper investigation.

In the past, sending out Requests for Proposals (RFPs) to software vendors was more commonplace, but in the current market, strong vendors—including those likely to be best for your needs—may choose not to take the substantial time required to answer an RFP when they don't know the likelihood that they'll win your business. If you have a very large project that will look particularly good in a vendor portfolio, or if your organization requires you to work with a conservative bidding process, sending out a shorter, more general Request for Information (RFI) might get the information you need without wasting your time and the vendors'.

For a costly purchase, consider seeking out a consultant to look at your organization's needs and offer software suggestions. Consultants often have a solid understanding of the current marketplace and can recommend the software packages most likely to fit your needs. An extra set of eyes can also be useful in determining software features your organization could use but may have overlooked. The added cost of hiring a consultant might be offset by purchasing a software package that will be right for your organization not just now, but as your needs evolve in the future as well. ●

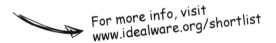 For more info, visit
www.idealware.org/shortlist

Evaluating Software

Once you have whittled down your list to the major contenders, it's time to begin working with vendors and demoing software. Vendors can help your mission reach new heights, or they can hold you back—it's important to take the time to learn everything you can about them, and about their software, before making a final decision.

Most vendors will be happy to provide a trial version or demo their product over the web, which makes it easy to see their systems in action. If a vendor is going to give you a guided tour, take some time beforehand to define the specific features and functions you want to see and send them to the vendor in advance. If you leave them to define their own tour of the product, you'll likely get a great view of the strengths that glosses over the weaknesses. They should be able to give you an overview of how the software meets the needs you care about—be cautious if a vendor seems to repeatedly misunderstand or talk around a question you've asked several times, and be sure to ask the vendor to clarify if you don't understand how something they've demoed meets the needs you asked about.

Don't get wrapped up in exploring features you may not need. Complex features and fancy graphics can seem engaging, especially when they're highlighted by the vendor, but you will learn more useful information about the software by running through the processes you most need. In the end, it doesn't matter what a system does if it doesn't do what you need it to.

To make the most out of your software purchase, you should also research vendors for specific information regarding their longevity in the marketplace. For example, how long have they been in business? How many of their clients are organizations similar to yours? An online search can reveal a lot about your vendor's history, including major changes to the company, litigations, and profitability.

Your relationship with a software vendor is one your organization will maintain for several years, so take the time to find not only software that works for your organization, but also a vendor that clicks with you. ●

 For more info, visit www.idealware.org/softwareeval

Comparing Open Source and Proprietary Software

Many organizations have strong feelings when it comes to comparing open source software to proprietary, vendor-supported options. Some advocate open source products (those built and supported by a community and then given away for free) as totally customizable, feature packed, and completely free software. Others believe that having a company behind a product, including the support and implementation help it can provide, makes proprietary, vendor-supported software the better bet. In practice, there's a lot of blurring between open source and proprietary software in today's market, and it probably makes sense to compare the options based on your own needs rather than assuming one model or the other will work better for you.

There are specific differences between the models, however. When purchasing proprietary software, a vendor will typically assist you in setting up and tweaking it to your needs, but you'll need to pay a sometimes-substantial fee and sign a contract. With an open source package, you simply download the software for free—but any installation, training, or customization is left up to you or to a hired consultant. There's no contract with an open source tool; you can start or stop using it at any time, but no contract means no warranties. It can be more challenging for organizations to troubleshoot bugs and hold developers accountable for problems with open source software.

If your organization has never used open source software before, it may be difficult to get it working perfectly right away, especially without hiring a consultant. Historically, many open source tools have been designed around what makes sense to developers rather than users, making them sometimes more difficult to use. Vendors for large proprietary software packages often have staff members trained to work with organizations from the ground up, which can be helpful—but which may make you reliant upon the vendor rather than your pick of qualified consultants for help.

This applies to support as well. Vendors often provide straight-forward support packages, but that's often your only option. You may need to devote more time to finding a consultant to support your open source implementation, but if you're not happy with one consultant, you can find another that better meets your needs. These days, in fact, some open source developers offer the same type of support, services, and even installation as a vendor, for a fee.

An open source tool by definition is open to modification by programmers, so you can make it do just about anything given sufficient time and money. Unless you're devoting a huge budget to your project, however, this probably isn't a practical path. Instead, look at what configuration options your software has, and what community-built add-ons are available. Open source tools typically are strong in both elements, but some specific proprietary tools are equally strong.

In general, your final choice shouldn't be based on whether a system is open source or proprietary, but on how well the features fit your needs and the total cost of the product. Many proprietary software vendors will provide free trials for their software so you can try them out alongside their open source competitors. Consider the cost of the time involved in setting up and learning any new software as well as the technical knowledge needed to maintain it. ●

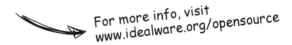

For more info, visit
www.idealware.org/opensource

Comparing Installed and Cloud Based Software

The term "cloud" has been a real buzzword lately, but cloud-based software goes by many names—and whatever you call it, it's here to stay. Hosted software, Software as a Service (SaaS), ASP Software, and On-Demand Software are different terms that usually refer to the same thing: software used in the cloud. Such systems can offer a variety of benefits, including easy maintenance and remote access, but give users less control over updates and require a reliable internet connection.

Typically, software used by an entire organization is purchased and installed on a server or on many computers at once. With cloud-based software, you pay a monthly fee, and any licensed member of your organization can access the software from anywhere with a speedy internet connection—in some cases, even on smartphones and tablets. Many respected software companies are making the switch to cloud-based options, and everything from online payment processing tools to full-blown donor management systems can be accessed this way.

One of the largest misconceptions surrounding cloud-based software is the lack of security. Since your data isn't stored on your computer, it's more liable to threats, right? Not at all—big software companies have the resources to back up your data, keep your software up to date, and protect you against threats often more effectively than a small organization could. Still, the company does have access to your data, and if you work with data that you might need to subpoena for—like case records for your work with Iraqi immigrants—an installed system might be the safest bet.

Most cloud-based software is paid for with a monthly or yearly subscription. It's similar to a "rent" vs. "own" model—it's likely to cost less upfront to rent cloud-based software, but the monthly subscription to use the software can add up over time. If you find you need to store a lot of data and allow many users to access it, you may be grateful you paid the one-time fee for installed software a few years down the line. Keep in mind, however, that you will also need to pay to buy and maintain the servers used to run an installed software.

Being online, cloud-based software can frequently integrate seamlessly with Broadcast Email, online donation tools, and websites. Additionally, most cloud-based software can work from anywhere—including from home or on the road—and can be accessed equally well with Windows, OSX, and Linux, provided you are using a compatible web browser.

Much of the work of a system administrator is left to the vendor with a cloud-based system. The vendor installs updates, maintains the servers, and monitors the system to keep it up and running so you don't have to. If you don't have any IT staff, this can be a huge benefit. However, this reduces the amount of control you have over the software. For example, the vendor may automatically roll out new features that might confuse your users.

In general, choose your software based not on whether it's cloud-based or installed, but on features and the total cost of the product. Weigh the desire to save money in the short term, and the need to pay someone to maintain an installed system, with the possible long-term cost savings of an installed system in the long run. And make sure you compare the software package carefully to your list of requirements—it doesn't matter if the software is installed or in the cloud if it doesn't do what you need it to do. ●

 For more info, visit www.idealware.org/cloud

Choosing a Consultant

Consultants can offer your organization a wide range of benefits. Perhaps you need a fresh perspective, some good advice, or just a little extra help during a busy time of year. If you understand your goals and determine what exactly is beyond your capabilities, an outside voice can help your organization surpass what it could do alone.

Your organization can gain a lot of valuable knowledge and first-hand experience from working with a consultant. If you are looking at improving your donor management system, for example, a consultant can impartially identify the weak points of your current setup and give you examples of how similar organizations have dealt with those problems. If your staff knows what they need but can't decide on a solution, a consultant can help define a process to weigh pros and cons and cut through internal politics. If you're heavily customizing a system or building one from scratch, bringing in a consultant will almost be a certainty.

To find a good consultant, start by asking other organizations for recommendations. State nonprofit associations, relevant email discussion lists, or groups that are focused on your cause can be other good sources for potential consultants.

Schedule a phone call with a number of consultants. Talk to them about the goals of your project, and what you envision as an end result, and ask them how they would achieve those objectives. They should be able to talk about one or more ways they could get to that end result and not just sell you on the big picture. Make sure you can understand what they're telling you—a consultant who can't speak language you understand is a red flag. Since your consultant will be a valuable member of your team, treat the interview and screening process seriously, and check references to hear about other people's experiences. ●

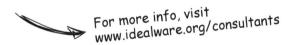

For more info, visit www.idealware.org/consultants

Evaluating Software Contracts

A contract with a software vendor can be a complicated document with terms and conditions you might not immediately understand. If you're purchasing a small piece of software from a vendor who deals with tens of thousands of clients, you may not be able to negotiate your contract, but you can always choose to walk away. There are some basic concepts you should be familiar with to ensure that your contract meets your needs, and not just the vendor's.

You should make sure that your vendor has included what course of action should to be taken if you have a problem. If the vendor has promised anything to you in the past, it must be included in the contract. For example, if the vendor promised that your software can be fully integrated with your Broadcast Email tool, and you find it doesn't live up to your expectations, the vendor should be legally obligated to work with you to find a solution. Additionally, you should make certain there are fair penalties for both you and your vendor in the event of small or major issues. If you cancel a consultation, for example, make sure that the fees for doing so are within reason, and that there is some recourse should they put you in the same position.

The software license is a major component of the contract. There should be no language implying that your access to data is restricted, or that your data can be used by the vendor in any way—outside of showing you your data inside the software. On the other hand, you should be able to do what you need with your data. If you are concerned that your use of the software may void the warranty, ask to have it changed. For a larger software purchase, contract negotiation is common and sometimes even expected. If the vendor is performing consulting work with your organization, the Scope of Work (SOW) is often an attachment to the contract that outlines what is being purchased, by whom, and for how much. It can also include a timeline for implementation of the software, or any other tasks to be completed by the vendor. In general, the more specific these outlines are the better.

Especially in the case of a large software purchase, you may want to consult with a contract attorney. ●

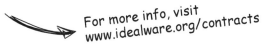

For more info, visit
www.idealware.org/contracts

Migrating Data

Moving data from one system to another, typically called "data migration," can be a long process. If you need to move complex data like accounting records, constituent data, or web pages, you'll need someone with significant experience working with databases to ensure a smooth transition. It's very rare for the data in one system to easily map into a new one; most of the time, there are complex considerations of where, precisely, to put all the information in your new system, and how to get it there. Most organizations will benefit from hiring a consultant for this process.

The length of time it will take to transfer your data is highly dependent on its current condition. If your organization has been keeping records for years without carefully managing them, your data may be out of date and full of erroneous and duplicated information, and pulling together and cleaning the data could take much longer than the process of actually moving the data. It's critical to clean the data before starting to use your new system. If this step is skipped, problems caused by bad data can heavily affect your staff's comfort with a new system. Cleaning the data in your old system is likely to be a much better plan than trying to fix it in your new one.

If your data is particularly messy, or the process of migration particularly complicated, consider carrying over only the most important data. While this clearly isn't ideal, it might boost confidence in your new database and save time in the long run to move only the data that you're sure is accurate and fill in the blanks over time when new information needs to be added. Some organizations, in fact, choose to keep both their old and their new systems running in parallel for a limited time, ensuring the old data will still be accessible until you no longer need it.

If you're planning to hire a consultant to transfer your data—which is often desirable—it's generally more valuable for them to thoroughly understand the ins and outs of your new system rather than your old one. Your new vendor can often suggest a good consultant for your needs. In working with them, try to be as specific as possible about your goals and expectations, and allow plenty of time for the switch to happen. If problems arise, new solutions and compromises may need to be agreed upon with the consultant.

Whatever method you choose, make sure that you do some trial runs of your data conversion before moving the data, and some serious spot checking of the data in its new location to ensure that data migration will be as painless as possible. ●

For more info, visit
www.idealware.org/data

Training and Supporting Staff

Training and support are one of the most important, but frequently overlooked, steps of implementing new software. It won't matter if you buy the most sophisticated software on the market if your staff doesn't know how to use it. Keeping your entire organization up to date will help to ensure that you are making the most out of your purchase.

To design your training, assess what you need from your system, including how it will affect each of your staff members and what processes will change. For example, is it worthwhile to train everyone in your office on how to enter event information into the system if you only have one event per year? Who is assigned to enter data, and how should it be entered? Who will need to know if something goes wrong?

When signing a contract for a new system, discuss how your nonprofit will be trained, and how much it will cost. Your software company will often have a training package to help you get to know the system inside-and-out. Alternatively, independent consultants can provide useful training that's often more tailored to your specific needs.

Don't plan to just train your staff once and assume they'll be experts forever. Regular refresher courses are important to maximizing productivity with your system. A lot of software designed for nonprofits can be complicated and packed with features not everyone will use daily. If you have many volunteers who work with your system, or a high rate of employee turnover, it's even more important to stay on top of training. Having a quick reference for the features your organization uses the most can be helpful for the entire staff.

In addition, it's important to know who your staff can turn to if they have a problem. Software vendors will usually offer support over the phone, by email, or over Skype—however, you shouldn't have to wait for customer service every time someone forgets how to print a report. If you don't have a dedicated technology guru, someone on your staff should be the one to go to with little problems, so things can keep moving smoothly. Consultants can also be helpful, especially if vendor-provided support is limited or non-existent. ●

For more info, visit
www.idealware.org/support

Caring for Your Data

To get the most out of your data, it's important to keep it organized. Many nonprofits suffer from unwieldy lists of donors, volunteers, and even accounting records. A little process refinement can make your data much more accessible and effective while making your life easier.

You should establish specific rules as to how to enter new data. If one volunteer enters "Mr." into the Title field, and another enters "Marketing Manager," it can be difficult to find what you need. Identify what information your organization absolutely needs for each record—for instance, is a record that only has an email address and no other information valuable, or should that person not be entered until there's more information?

It's also important to define the timeframe for entry—should a check be entered into the database within an hour? A day? A month? These kinds of rules not only keep your data clean, but ensure that everyone is on the same page as to what to expect from the data. Once you define the rules, make sure you let everyone know what's expected. This will likely require not just a one-off training, but periodic refreshers.

Making sure you know who can access and enter data will help as well. It's critical to ensure that one person is accountable for the quality of your data, but you'll likely want multiple people to be able to access it. It's a balancing act to ensure that you allow access to the people who really need it, but not so many that there's a lot of possibility of error or duplication.

It's also critical to set up a periodic process to check in on and clean your data. In addition to checking for duplicates and errors, outdated information may need to be deleted. Define when a constituent record is no longer useful to your organization—for instance, if a constituent is deceased or hasn't been active in years, should you delete or archive them? An unwieldy system full of everyone your organization has ever interacted with over 50 years is going to slow down your staff's ability to quickly get what they need. ●

For more info, visit www.idealware.org/datacare

Want to learn more? In this section, you'll find a list of websites where you can get more helpful resources, information about the authors and reviewers who made this Field Guide possible, and an index in which you can look up all the different types of systems discussed in these pages.

TechSoup *www.techsoup.org*

 TechSoup.org offers nonprofits a one-stop resource for technology needs by providing free information, resources, and discounted software. They provide instructional articles and worksheets for nonprofit staff members who make use of information technologies, as well as technology planning information for executives and other decision makers. In addition, their TechSoup Stock program offers more than 600 donated and discounted products at very low administrative fees.

NTEN *www.nten.org*

NTEN is the membership organization of nonprofit professionals who put technology to use for their causes. They bring together a community of peers who share technology solutions across the sector and support each other's work. They enable members to embrace advances in technology through knowledge-sharing, trainings, research, and industry analysis.

Aspiration *http://www.aspirationtech.org/*

Aspiration helps nonprofits and foundations use software tools more effectively and sustainably. They serve as ally, coach, strategist, mentor, and facilitator to those trying to make more impactful use of information technology in their social change efforts. ●

About Idealware

Idealware, a 501(c)(3) nonprofit, provides thoroughly researched, impartial, and accessible resources about software to help nonprofits make smart software decisions.

Nonprofits maintain a complicated relationship with technology. Most know that software can streamline their processes and help fulfill their missions more efficiently and effectively, yet lean staffing and tight budgets mean they're unable to devote the time necessary to keep up with new technologies and find the right tools.

From the most basic questions, like how to use software to help manage emailing hundreds of people at once, to the more complex, like understanding the role of social networking and mobile phone text-messaging in fundraising strategy, organizations need a trusted source for answers.

By synthesizing vast amounts of original research into credible and approachable information, Idealware helps nonprofits make the most of their time and financial resources. And our reach is expanding. Our reports have been downloaded hundreds of thousands of times.

Along with reports and articles, Idealware also gets into the trenches with nonprofits through our interactive online training. Each month we create a training theme to give your organization a broad look at technology topics, including social media, fundraising, and back office operations. These 90-minute seminars get rave reviews from the participants, but we take the training a step further with our Toolkits. Made up of five or six 90-minute sessions, Idealware's Toolkits offer extremely detailed training on one topic, including email fundraising, advanced social media, and website development. Along with the training, participants have access to an Idealware expert during weekly office hours. To round out the learning opportunities, Idealware offers the only training of its kind in our On Demand Tactical Technology Planning. Made up of five units and 26 modules, On Demand Tactical

Tech Planning allows participants to take the training at their own pace on the device of their choice. When completed, they'll have complete tactical technology plans for their organizations.

To join any of Idealware's trainings, visit our website at www.idealware.org. To learn more about On Demand Tactical Tech Planning, visit tacticaltech.idealware.org.

Who's behind Idealware? Idealware is made up of a small, growing staff aided by a community of experts, including content partners and contributors, and overseen by a remarkable board or directors and set of advisors.

Want to connect with us? Join the conversation on Twitter or Facebook.

Twitter: @idealware

Facebook: facebook.com/Idealware

Laura Quinn

As Idealware's Executive Director, Laura leads Idealware's activities. Prior to Idealware, Laura founded Alder Consulting, where she helped nonprofits create internet strategies, select appropriate software, and then build sophisticated websites on a limited budget. Laura is a frequent speaker and writer on nonprofit technology topics.

Chris Bernard

Chris is Idealware's Editorial and Communications Director. Prior to joining Idealware, he worked in journalism, advertising, marketing communications, and as a technical writer.

Elizabeth Pope

Elizabeth is Director of Research and Operations, and directs Idealware's software research projects. She worked in archives and libraries in New York City, and her background also includes fundraising and content development for nonprofit organizations.

Kyle Henri Andrei

As Research Analyst, Kyle is responsible for researching software through demos, interviews, and surveys, and using that information to create Idealware's reports and articles.

Tyler M. Cummins

As Marketing and Learning Associate, Tyler manages Idealware's presence online and lends a creative eye to all things training. He began his life at Idealware as a research intern. ●

Many thanks to the nonprofit staff and consultants who contributed to this and previous editions of the Field Guide.

Andrea Berry
Hardy Girls Healthy Women

Steven Backman
Database Design Associates

Marc Baizman
My Computer Guy Consulting

Johanna Bates
Johanna Bates Consulting

Alex Brant-Zawadzki
Organizing for America

Matthew Burnett
Pro Bono Net

Ferran Busquets, Arrels Fundació
Peter Campbell
Earthjustice

Jonathan Cass
Animal Humane Society

Marion Conway
Marion Conway Consulting

Peter Davis
Free Flow Data

Kate Dillon
Save The Bay

Judith Freeman
New Organizing Institute

Heather Gardner-Madras
gardner-madras | strategic creative

Heidi Genrich
Causecast.org

Matt Koltermann
Action Against Hunger

Kaitlin LaCasse
Former Idealware VISTA

Eric Leland
FivePaths, LLC

Timo Luege
International Federation of Red Cross and Red Crescent Societies

Heather Mason
A Caspian Production

Michelle Murrain
OpenIssue, LLC

Rowan Price
Free Flow Digital

Matt Reading
Alaska Wilderness League

Norman Reiss
Nonprofit Bridge

Mark Sansone
See3 Communications

David Silversmith
First Book

Michael Stein
DonorDigital

Karen Taggert
PETA Foundation

Thomas Taylor
Greater Philadelphia Cultural Alliance

Mal Warwick
DonorDigital

Ken Williams
AED Center for Leadership Development

Robert Weiner
Robert L. Weiner Consulting

Ron Zucker
Kelley Campaigns

Usha Venkatachallam
Appropriate IT

Steve Birnbaum
JCA

Jason Lefkowitz
Rogue Repairman

Walt Daniels
NY/NJ Trail Conference

Maddie Grant
SocialFish

Eve Fox
M+R Strategic Services

Tracy Betts
Balance Interactive

Chris Tuttle
Tuttle Communications

Idealware also wishes to thank Dawn Lovelace, Naomi Adler Dancis, and Jeff Hannon for their contributions to the 2014 Field Guide.

A

B

C

D

E

To learn more about this Field Guide, or about
co-branding it for your own network, go to

www.idealware.org/fieldguide

Made in the USA
Lexington, KY
28 July 2014